CW00666210

Wimp Programming for All

Lee Calcraft and Alan Wrigley

Published by
RISC Developments Ltd, St Albans
October 1992

Wimp Programming for All

Lee Calcraft and Alan Wrigley

© RISC Developments Ltd. 1992
ISBN 1-85142-088-6
First edition October 1992

All rights reserved. No part of this book or any of the programs to which it relates may be reproduced or translated in any form, by any means, mechanical, electronic or otherwise, without the prior written consent of the publisher.

Disclaimer: Neither the publisher nor the authors can accept any liability as to the suitability or accuracy of any information, or of the programs on the associated disc, for any given application. No liability can be accepted for any consequential loss or damage however caused arising from the use of the advice or programs contained in this book, or from the use of any program on the associated disc.

This book was produced entirely on an Acorn Archimedes. It was written and edited using RISC Developments' *DeskEdit* program and text editor, and typeset using the same publisher's *Ovation* DTP package.

Published by RISC Developments Ltd, 117 Hatfield Road, St Albans, Herts AL1 4JS.
Telephone (0727) 40303, Fax (0727) 860263.

Printed and bound in the UK by Arlon House, Kings Langley, Herts

Contents

Appendices

Introduction

Welcome to the Wimp. This book has been written to satisfy the need for a straightforward explanation of the techniques involved in programming Acorn's Window Manager (known as the Wimp), as provided on the Archimedes and other computers using Acorn's RISC OS operating system. Henceforward, this book will use the generic names "Archimedes" and "Arc" to refer to all computers within these ranges, unless specifically stated otherwise.

This book is suitable for all Archimedes users who are interested in writing multi-tasking Wimp-based programs for the computer. Some prior knowledge of programmming in BBC Basic is assumed, as well as a familiarity with the RISC OS Desktop from a user's point of view (clicking, dragging, choosing menu options, opening and closing windows etc.). However, one of the aims of the book is to show that simple and effective Wimp programs can easily be written by non-expert programmers once the basic principles of the interface are understood.

Wimp Programming for All will take you step by step through the concepts and practicalities of Wimp programming in a clear and logical fashion. The text is backed up at all stages by program listings designed to illustrate the techniques being described. Each of these listings, when added to the existing program as described in the book, will make up a complete application which demonstrates the points being introduced in the text. All these listings, together with the complete applications in each case, are provided on the associated disc which is available separately. The text and program examples in this book are equally applicable to both RISC OS 2 and RISC OS 3, unless specifically stated otherwise.

The programming language used for the examples given in the book is BBC Basic, since this is widely used by programmers and, being available in the computer from the moment it is switched on, provides an effective way to harness the power of the Arc without expense or effort. However, the techniques covered in the book are equally applicable to other languages such as C or Assembler. C is especially suitable for programming the Wimp; Acorn's implementation of C has been optimised for that purpose, with many Wimp-specific routines provided. Many commercial RISC OS applications are written in C, and readers who wish to write more substantial Wimp-based programs are encouraged to investigate the use of C to do so.

CONVENTIONS

All program listings in this book are displayed in the Courier typeface (e.g. `5020 SYS "Hourglass_On"`), and are taken from tested and working programs. In the text, all Basic keywords are written wholly in capitals (e.g. REPEAT, ELSE, TRUE), while references to certain keys on the keyboard are given an initial capital letter (e.g. Return, Shift, Ctrl etc.). Italics are used to add emphasis to words, to distinguish menu items, icon legends and the like from normal text, or to introduce a word which has a specific meaning in the context of Wimp programming. This style is also used for variable names, but only where they appear in normal text so that they may be more readily identified in that context.

Two keyboard characters which sometimes cause confusion and which may appear in program listings are underline (or underscore) and vertical bar. The former is above the hyphen on the keyboard and appears in print as _ while the latter is on the key above Return and appears as |.

You should also be careful to differentiate in listings between `0` (zero) and `O` (upper case O), and between `1` (one) and `l` (lower case L). A further common source of problems when typing in listings is failure to spot multiple commas, particularly in SYS statements.

Wimp programming makes frequent use of blocks of memory for parameter passing. In discussing the principles, the address of such a memory area will be given in the style 'block', but in all program examples the equivalent variable *block%* will be used as in the usual convention.

THE ASSOCIATED DISC

To accompany this book there is a separate disc containing all the program fragments listed in the book, together with the complete applications which are built up from these fragments, and additional supporting programs.

The disc may only be obtained direct from the publishers for £4.95 inc. VAT plus £1 p&p. See Appendix E for more details of the contents of this disc.

FURTHER RESOURCES

A number of useful resources are available for the Wimp programmer. Foremost among these is Acorn's *Programmer's Reference Manual* (PRM). This is really the Archimedes programmer's bible, since it details all aspects of the operating system and how to access it from your own programs. Acorn's open approach to this interaction between programmer and machine contrasts very favourably with other computer systems where the operating system is a closed book, understood only by a few dedicated gurus. This willingness on the part of Acorn to document every aspect of its operating system, and furthermore to make much of it accessible to other programmers, is what makes the Archimedes such a delightful and flexible computer to program.

The PRM, then, should be considered essential if you want to progress beyond the basic concepts covered by this book. You will also find that there are a number of useful programming utilities available from various sources which will make life easier when writing your own programs, for example to help you design the windows which your program will use, or to aid in debugging when things go wrong. RISC Developments' *Wimp Programmer's Toolkit* was compiled with this in mind, and contains a number of powerful utilities which will be a great help to any Wimp programmer (Appendix F gives details). Readers will find that a good text and program editor (such as RISC Developments' *DeskEdit*) can also be invaluable in writing and editing programs.

ACKNOWLEDGEMENTS

The basis for this book is Lee Calcraft's excellent series of articles entitled Mastering the Wimp which appeared in RISC User magazine (from September 1989 to May 1991). However, the original articles have been greatly expanded and much new material has been added to ensure that this book provides a complete solution for those who wish to get to grips with programming the Wimp.

Alan Wrigley
October 1992

1. Introducing the Wimp

What is the Wimp? - Multi-tasking - Wimp applications - SWI calls - Outline of a Wimp program - Application directories - An example program - Introduction to error handling

WHAT IS THE WIMP?

The first question asked by many newcomers to the Archimedes is "What on earth is the Wimp"? Is there a weak little man inside the computer who is programmed to do whatever you ask without complaint?

In fact WIMP is an acronym, originally standing for Windows, Icons, Mouse and Pull-down menus, reflecting the fact that the earliest Wimp interfaces featured menus which were "pulled down" with the mouse pointer from a bar at the top of the screen. Nowadays WIMP is generally taken to stand for Windows, Icons, Menus and Pointer, which in any case makes more sense in the Archimedes environment since RISC OS menus may appear anywhere on the screen and are not "pull-down" in nature.

When we speak of "the Wimp" in an Archimedes context, we are in fact referring to the Acorn Window Manager, which is a resident module within the RISC OS operating system. The Wimp is an example of what is known as a Graphical User Interface (GUI). Broadly speaking, this means that the information presented to the user about actions and options which are available is represented in a graphical form, and may be selected by using the mouse to point and click, as opposed to older style programs which communicated by displaying text on the screen and expected the user in turn to type text at a prompt to give the computer instructions.

The very name of the Wimp describes the kind of GUI which it is; a program running under the Wimp uses windows on the screen, and icons within these windows, to display information. An icon is simply a box of any size containing text, a picture or both, which can be placed anywhere within the window. The user interacts with the program by using the mouse to move the pointer around the screen, and to click over specific icons and/or windows to communicate with the program, while options open to the user are available from menus.

The Acorn Wimp is a very powerful and comprehensive piece of software available and accessible to all Archimedes users. Most importantly of all, it provides the means by which full co-operative multi-tasking is achieved on machines with RISC OS fitted.

MULTI-TASKING

The ability to multi-task is really the key to understanding why we should want to learn to program the Wimp. Multi-tasking means quite simply that more than one software application can be active in your computer at the same time, and furthermore all these applications can not only share access to resources such as filing systems and printers, but also transfer data directly between each other. If the Archimedes is your first computer you may take this facility for granted, but until very recently the idea of multi-tasking on a personal computer would have seemed like a dream to most users.

This, then, is the prime reason for writing programs which make use of the Wimp, since multi-tasking is not possible without it. But the Wimp also greatly simplifies access to filing systems. If your program needs to operate on data files, you do not need to write any code to find files or display information about them, or move around the directory structure of disc or network systems. The Desktop filer provides all this, and allows you to drag data files into an application in order to load them - and much more besides.

WIMP APPLICATIONS

In the three years or so since Acorn first introduced RISC OS, a bewildering variety of applications have appeared on the market which make full use of its facilities. Most importantly of all, hardly anyone now writes non-multi-tasking programs for the Arc, a fact which in itself indicates how powerful and all-embracing the concept of the Wimp has become. Almost anything a computer can do is a candidate for a multi-tasking application, and it is worth considering some typical examples of these at this point in order to illustrate the range of what can be achieved, and perhaps to whet your appetite for developing your own ideas.

At the bottom end of the scale, magazines regularly publish small Basic programs contributed by readers which perform simple but useful tasks, for example Desktop calculators, clocks, diaries and a whole host of other ideas. All these are well within the scope of a relative newcomer to Wimp programming, and all are ideally suited to multi-tasking operation.

Higher up the ladder are commercial programs performing specific operations which, on their own, may be of limited use, but when used in conjunction with other applications running alongside them in the machine, open up a world of possibilities which are impossible or difficult to achieve on a single-tasking computer. For example, a graph plotter can accept data input from one application, perhaps in the form of text, turn it into a pictorial graph in any one of a number of formats, and output it into an art package or a desktop publisher to form part of a larger document. Once upon a time this would only have been possible by running the three applications separately one by one, saving the data away to a file each time, and then quitting so that the next application could be run. This would then load the file in turn, process it and so on.

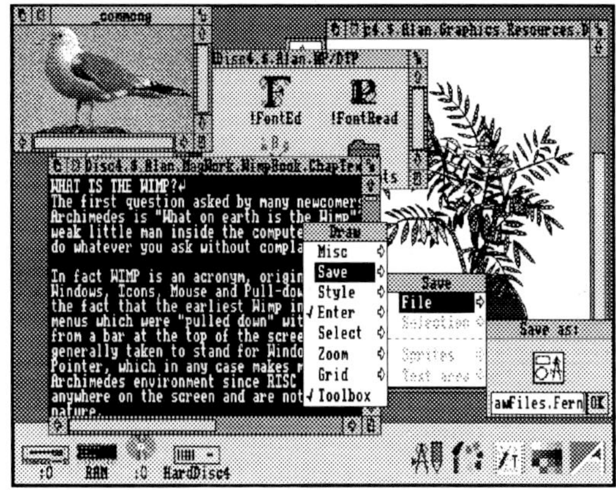

Applications multi-tasking on the RISC OS Desktop

Along with these purely software applications, there are programs which support hardware devices, such as scanners, digitisers and sound samplers, all producing resources which can be used by other applications while running alongside them in the multi-tasking environment.

Finally, there are applications which perform a major task, and which may interact with several other applications along the way, either to import or to export data in any one of a number of different forms. We have already mentioned art and desktop publishing packages; we could add spreadsheets, databases, music packages and so on.

What this means for the average programmer is that programs do not have to be large or complex to be of use. Provided that the guidelines laid down by Acorn are closely followed (and this book will do its best to encourage you to do so), small programs can have a vital role to play in the chain; with multi-tasking it is no longer necessary for every program to re-invent the wheel.

The only real disadvantage from the programmer's point of view is the complexity of the Wimp, but this is really quite unavoidable in view of the massive flexibility built into the system, as we will see in due course. Indeed, in some cases the complexity of the system actually works to the programmer's advantage. For example, if you were writing a program without the Wimp, you would need to include routines to display text in the correct place on the screen each time it is required, and to handle text typed in by the user. The latter may involve filtering out unacceptable characters, detecting the cursor being moved around the text and so on. But with the Wimp, all you have to do is create a text icon, and the Wimp itself handles text input and output to that icon automatically.

Furthermore, because every multi-tasking program must communicate with the Wimp in the same way, there are a number of core routines which can be common to all programs. Once you have written a "shell" program containing these routines (for which Basic is a perfectly acceptable language), this can be used as the basis for every multi-tasking program you will ever write (in fact, the accompanying disc contains just such a set of routines to help you get started). The point we are making is that although the Wimp is complex, you need have no fears about learning to program it, and once you have mastered the basics (which is the purpose of this book), you will actually find programming easier than without it.

INTRODUCING THE WIMP

Because of the complexity of the Wimp, we will be treating the whole subject in a progressive fashion, with the intention of spreading the introduction of new concepts throughout the book. To make this possible, we will gloss over a number of areas early on, returning to them at a later date to fill in the gaps. Don't get disheartened if at first it all seems a little daunting. If you re-read any sections which are unclear, and study the program listings carefully and experiment with them, you will soon find that programming the Wimp becomes second nature.

So let's now get down to brass tacks. Put very simply, a program which wishes to multi-task must first register itself with the Wimp. It must create any windows and icons which it needs for itself, load in any files containing essential resources, and then for the rest of its life it must sit patiently in the computer repeatedly asking the Wimp to tell it when the user has performed an action which requires its attention. This might be clicking the mouse over an icon or typing in some text, for example. To do this it must strike up a dialogue with the Wimp. In due course we will see how to do all of these things.

SWI CALLS

Virtually all access to the Wimp is via so-called SWI calls. SWI stands for SoftWare Interrupt, and is the method by which calls are made to routines inside the operating system or a module. SWI calls are made from Basic by using the SYS command. The rest of this section will give some details on how to use the SYS command; if you are already familiar with its use you can move on to the section entitled "WIMP SWI CALLS".

Although some simple Basic programs make no recourse to SWI calls, there are many operations which cannot be performed without their use. The Wimp is a case in point, being accessed almost exclusively via such calls. The Archimedes has a potential 16777216 such calls in its repertoire, though only a relatively small number are actually defined. Each SWI call has an identification number, and if you are in Basic, then each may also be referred to by name. For example the two calls:

```
SYS "OS_WriteC"
```

and

```
SYS 0
```

are equivalent. Most SWI calls also require parameters to be passed, and this is done by setting up the ARM processor's registers before making the call. There are 15 such registers, normally referred to as R0-R15. If you were writing in machine code, you would need to place the correct values into the appropriate registers before making the SWI call, but Basic's SYS command does it all for you at the time of making the call; all you have to do is specify the parameters in the correct order, starting with R0, and separated by commas, and they will be put into the correct registers. In other words, the first parameter in the list will be passed in R0, and so on.

As an example, consider the SWI **OS_WriteC** which we have just met. The effect of this call is to output a single character to the current VDU stream (normally the screen). The character to be output must be supplied as a parameter in R0. To output the letter *A* for example, you would write:

```
SYS "OS_WriteC",65
```

since 65 is the ASCII code for *A*.

Generally speaking it is always best to supply the SWI name rather than its number, since this makes your code easier to follow. But if you *are* using the name, it must be entered exactly as it appears, right down to the case of each letter. If you entered the name as **Os_WriteC** you would get the error *No such SWI*. You should also be careful with the underscore character used in all SWI names. This is produced by pressing Shift together with the minus key. Note also the vitally important comma separating the name and the first parameter. If you miss this out a syntax error will be signalled.

In practice almost all SWI calls take one or more parameters. For example, **OS_Plot** takes 3:

```
SYS "OS_Plot",4,100,200
```

This call would move the graphics cursor to point 100,200 (4 is the plot code for *move absolute*). Sometimes you will see that one or more parameters have been omitted from a call by placing the separating commas adjacent to each other. Usually this is done when the value in a particular register is not relevant, but a value in a subsequent register *is*. When a value is not specified, the operating system inserts a value of zero in the corresponding ARM register.

In these examples the parameters we have passed are treated as four-byte integer values, since each register can contain one four-byte word. But sometimes it is necessary to pass a pointer to a string in one of the registers. The SYS command handles this quite neatly for you. All you have to do is to pass the actual string itself, or the name of the string, as the parameter, and Basic will calculate the address of that string and pass it on with the SWI call. For example, the SWI **OS_WriteN** sends a string to the current output stream. R0 contains a pointer to the string while R1 contains the number of bytes to send. This could be achieved in Basic in the following way:

```
text$="Hello world"
SYS "OS_WriteN",text$,LEN(text$)
```

or simply:

```
SYS "OS_WriteN","Hello world",11
```

Sometimes when large quantities of information must be passed to a SWI routine, a so-called *parameter block* is used. This happens with most Wimp calls. In such cases, the user builds up a data block in RAM containing the information needed by the SWI, and then passes the start address of the block as one of the parameters of the call. For example, **OS_Word** with R0=15 writes information to the computer's real-time clock. The information must be placed into a parameter block, the address of which is passed in R1. So you would make the call in the following way:

```
SYS "OS_Word",15,block%
```

having first dimensioned an area of memory starting at *block%* and placed into it the information required by the SWI routine.

SWI calls can also return information. **OS_Mouse** for example, returns the pointer x and y co-ordinates, the state of the mouse buttons and the time of button change, in the first four registers respectively. It might be used as follows:

```
SYS "OS_Mouse" TO x%,y%,button%,time%
```

Here, as in all cases where no parameters are supplied, the comma after the name may be omitted. After this call, the four variables following the keyword TO will hold the values returned by the call. As with the parameters supplied by the user, the return parameters reflect the contents of ARM registers R0, R1, R2 etc. And again, if a particular register in a sequence is to be ignored, the comma separators can be moved together. Thus the statement:

```
SYS "OS_Mouse" TO ,,button%
```

would still return the button state.

Finally, to illustrate how supplied and return parameters are used together, the following **OS_Byte** call will read CMOS RAM location *n%*, and store the result in the variable *result%*:

```
SYS "OS_Byte",161,n% TO ,,result%
```

Note the two commas before the variable *result%*, indicating that the value returned in this variable should be the contents of ARM register R2 (R0 and R1 being discarded). To test this out, try it with n%=134. The variable *result%* will return the size of the font cache (in units of 4K) configured in your machine.

All SWI calls which are described in this book will be printed in bold type wherever they appear. A list of all these calls is given in Appendix D. Full details on all the operating system's SWI calls, including parameters for each call, are given in the PRM.

WIMP SWI CALLS

RISC OS 2 has 52 Wimp SWI calls documented in the PRM, and RISC OS 3 has a total of 54. In the course of the book we will describe about half of these (listed in Appendix D), but initially in the first three chapters we will concentrate on just nine of the more common calls (see Figure 1.1).

Wimp_Initialise	Wimp_Poll
Wimp_CreateWindow	Wimp_CloseDown
Wimp_OpenWindow	Wimp_ReportError
Wimp_CloseWindow	Wimp_ProcessKey
Wimp_GetWindowState	

Figure 1.1
Some commonly used Wimp SWI calls

PARAMETER BLOCKS

As we mentioned earlier, most Wimp SWI calls require a parameter block, a pointer to which is usually passed in R1. For the majority of purposes the same block can be used for each call (though there are a few circumstances where it is necessary or advisable to use a different block, as we shall see). The Wimp requires the main block to be at least 256 bytes long, and it may need to be larger if it is going to be used to create a window whose definition requires more than 256 bytes. It is usual to dimension this block at the start of the program using the DIM statement, as in the following example:

```
DIM block% 255
```

Basic will set up the variable *block%* (the name is determined by the user) to point to a reserved area of 256 bytes. This would normally be done in a procedure which performs all the necessary initialisation routines.

INITIALISING A TASK

In very broad terms, a Wimp program will begin by making a call to SWI **Wimp_Initialise**. This informs the Wimp of the existence of the new task (or program). The Wimp replies by issuing the task with a so-called *task handle*. This is a number unique to that particular task, which may be used when referring to the task in future dialogues. Figure 1.2 shows the details of the parameters which should be passed to **Wimp_Initialise**, together with the information returned by the call.

On Entry:
R0 = Last Wimp version number *100 (at least 200)
R1 = "TASK" (low byte="T", high byte="K")
R2 = Pointer to description of task

On Exit:
R0 = Current Wimp version number *100
R1 = Task handle

Figure 1.2
Parameters for
SWI "Wimp_Initialise" (&400C0)

R0 should hold a value which represents the latest version of the Window Manager known to the task (200 for RISC OS 2 and 300 for RISC OS 3), R1 should hold the word TASK (literally - see below), while the third parameter (in R2) supplies a brief description of the task for the Task Manager display (for example, "Edit", "Paint" or "OurTask"). On exit R0 and R1 will hold respectively the version number of the Window Manager, and the task handle which it has assigned to the task.

The parameter supplied to R1 by the user is a little unusual in that it is not a *pointer* to a text string (as would normally be the case) but the text string itself, which has a value (in hex) of &4B534154. This is simply a little ruse to filter out tasks written for a pre-RISC OS version of the Window Manager, which would be very unlikely to pass that particular value in R1 when initialising.

Having made this call, the program may then perform any other necessary initialisation procedures. This may include loading any data which it requires at the outset, or creating windows for use in the program. We shall see how to do the latter in the next chapter.

THE WIMP POLL LOOP

Having done everything necessary to set itself up, the program must then enter a loop within which it repeatedly asks the Wimp for a progress report, and the Wimp in turn tells it when an action has occurred which requires its attention.

In all Wimp programs this loop must take the form of a central routine which makes repeated calls to **Wimp_Poll**. We will cover the use of **Wimp_Poll** fully in Chapter 3, but briefly, the Wimp responds to these calls by returning a value, called the *reason code*, to the calling program (or task), and the task in turn responds to this. The reason code indicates what kind of action has occurred that requires the task's attention; perhaps the user has clicked on an icon in the task's window, or has typed at the keyboard, or whatever. In any case, it is up to the task to interpret the reason code, react accordingly, and then call **Wimp_Poll** again to find out what to do next.

As far as the task is concerned, a call to **Wimp_Poll** simply invokes a response at some point from the Wimp. Unbeknown to the task, however, the Wimp uses this call to multi-task. What happens is that the Wimp returns to each task in turn, so that in the time between a task calling **Wimp_Poll**, and getting back a reason code, the Wimp has serviced each of the other concurrent tasks one by one. This is all handled completely by the Wimp, and all that each task must do is to call **Wimp_Poll** in a central

REPEAT loop, and to respond as quickly as possible to the reason code which the Wimp returns. It must then call **Wimp_Poll** again, so passing control back to the Window Manager. All Wimp programs must behave in this way, and no special code over and above this is needed to accomplish multi-tasking.

We can see, therefore, that multi-tasking works in the following way: your task initialises itself, then calls **Wimp_Poll** and sits back to await further instructions while other activities may be going on elsewhere in the computer. When an action occurs which needs to be processed by your task, the Wimp responds to your call and passes control to you. Your program must then deal with the action as quickly as possible (during which time it has sole control of the computer), and then pass control back to the Wimp. At all other times the Wimp has no need to trouble your task, and will get on with the job of servicing all the other active tasks in the same way. If you find that this is all a little unclear at this stage it is worth re-reading the above section until you have grasped it fully, since it is the key to the way in which the whole process of multi-tasking operates.

TERMINATING A TASK

Each task will have its own way of determining when the user wishes to quit (normally by providing a *Quit* option on the task's menu, selection of which will be notified to the task by the Wimp). When this time comes, the task must exit by calling **Wimp_CloseDown** which tells the Wimp that it no longer wishes to be active. This call only requires parameters in special cases, and for normal applications (such as those described in this book) these are not necessary.

APPLICATION DIRECTORIES

Before we go on to bring all these concepts we have introduced so far into a program for you to experiment with, we need to explain briefly the structure of a Wimp application. If you are familiar with application directories you may skip this and move on to the section entitled "A SIMPLE PROGRAM".

When you open up a directory display on the Desktop, you may see a variety of objects. There may be simple files, usually represented by square icons with a black border; some of these icons will probably be familiar to you, such as those for text or sprite files, for example. You may see directories, represented by pale blue icons in the shape of a folder. There may also be applications, which are characterised by the "!" in front of the name (in Acorn terminology this character is referred to as "pling" rather

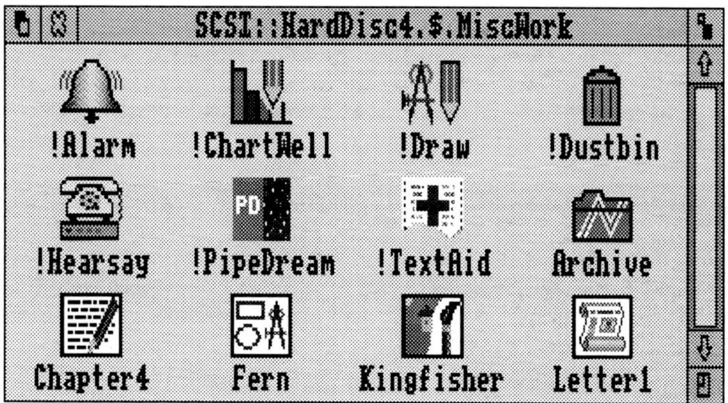

A directory display containing files and applications

than "exclamation mark"), and usually also by their own individual icon. What you are seeing is in fact an *application directory*, which RISC OS distinguishes from a conventional directory by the "!" character as the initial character of the name. The rest of the directory name usually reflects the name of the application itself - Edit's application directory, for example, is called *!Edit*. Incidentally, you should always refer to applications themselves by their name, e.g. *Edit*, *Ovation* and so on. *!Edit* or *!Ovation* should only be used when referring specifically to the application directory.

An application directory contains all the individual files and resources needed by the application in order to run. A full description of these is given in Appendix B, but for now you simply need to know that the main program (i.e. the one which contains the code that performs the application's functions) is always called *!RunImage*, and that there must be at least one other file in the application directory, which is an Obey file called *!Run*. The reason for this latter file is that when you double-click on an application directory (which is of course the standard method of running an application), RISC OS looks inside the directory for a file called *!Run*, and executes it. This process allows the application to set up various parameters before the main program is run. For example, a common function of the *!Run* file is to ask the Wimp to allocate a specific amount of memory to the application. The last action of the *!Run* file is usually to run *!RunImage*. *!RunImage* itself can be a Basic program, an ARM code program created using C or Assembler, or indeed a program in any language which is recognised by the computer.

From now on, we will assume that each time you type in a listing from this book, you will save it as *!RunImage* within an application directory. First of all, you will need to create an application directory for this purpose. To do this, simply choose the *New directory* option from a Filer menu, and type in a name of your choice beginning with "!". We will adopt the name *OurTask* for the application which we will build up throughout the book, so if you want to follow this course you should create a directory called *!OurTask*.

You will notice two things about this directory. Firstly, the icon which represents it is the standard pale blue and yellow "APP" icon. This is the default icon for application directories. You can create your own sprite for this icon to be used in place of the default, and details are given in Appendix B, but for the moment the default icon will do just as well. Secondly, because double-clicking on an application directory runs the application, you cannot open the directory by this method as with other directories. Instead, you must hold down Shift while double-clicking.

You must also create a *!Run* file. The easiest way to do this is to use Edit and choose the *Create New Obey file* option from the icon bar menu. For the moment this file need only contain two lines, as follows:

```
WimpSlot -min 32K -max 32K
Run <Obey$Dir>.!RunImage
```

Having typed in these two lines, open up the *!OurTask* directory as described above and save the file inside it with the name *!Run*. The purpose of these lines is explained more fully in Appendix B, but for now all you need to know is that the *WimpSlot* command requests a specific allocation of memory (in this case 32K), while the *Run* command runs the *!RunImage* program.

Now you have a skeleton application, and each time you create or modify a program from one of the listings in the book, you can save it inside the *!OurTask* directory as *!RunImage*. Double-clicking on *!OurTask* will then run the program.

A SIMPLE PROGRAM

To get you started without any further ado, Listing 1.1 contains a very simple program for you to type in which illustrates the calls described so far in this book. The program cannot really serve any useful purpose, since we have not yet covered the creation of windows. All that it does, therefore, is to initialise itself, call **Wimp_Poll**, generate an error the first time a reason code is returned, and then close down immediately.

In later chapters we will be building on this simple program as we go along, adding routines to illustrate the various elements of a multi-tasking program as they are described in the text. These routines can later be used as a framework for developing your own Wimp programs. Because the program will be regularly updated in this way, when you type in Listing 1.1, and all subsequent additions to this listing, you should adhere to the line numbering given, since we may need to refer to some of these lines at a later stage, and in any event many additional lines will eventually be inserted into what is for now just a skeleton framework.

Where program lines are given in the text, and are not part of a listing (i.e. they do not appear under the heading of "Listing n.n") then they are intended only as suggestions for you to experiment with, and subsequent listings will not necessarily assume that they have been included as part of the program.

When subsequent additions to the program are listed in the book, it may not always be easy to see the purpose of the new lines when viewed out of context with what is already in the program. For this reason, we recommend that whenever you add lines to the program, you list that whole section of the program in order to gain a better understanding of what exactly is going on.

Listing 1.1

```
 10 REM >!RunImage
 20 REM Wimp test program "OurTask"
 30 REM Updated to Chapter 1
 60 :
 70 PROCinit
 80 :
 90 WHILE NOT quit%
100 PROCpoll
110 ENDWHILE
120 SYS "Wimp_CloseDown"
130 END
140 :
150 DEF PROCinit
160 DIM block% 255
170 quit%=FALSE:app$="OurTask"
180 SYS "Wimp_Initialise",200,&4B534154,app$
480 ENDPROC
```

```
490 :
500 DEF PROCpoll
510 SYS "Wimp_Poll",0,block% TO reason%
520 CASE reason% OF
530 WHEN 0:PROCerror("This program does nothing usefu
l")
540 quit%=TRUE
670 ENDCASE
680 ENDPROC
690 :
700 DEF PROCerror(err$)
730 !block%=255
740 $(block%+4)=err$+CHR$0
750 SYS "Wimp_ReportError",block%,1,app$
760 ENDPROC
```

Since this is our very first program, it is worth looking at in a little detail. First of all *PROCinit* is called. It is usual for a program to have a procedure such as this, which performs all the necessary initialisation functions before **Wimp_Poll** is called for the first time. Line 160 reserves the block of memory which we need for any SWI call parameters, and also sets up a variable *quit%* which will be used to detect when the program should terminate. In line 180 you will see the call to **Wimp_Initialise**, exactly as described earlier. The program then enters the poll loop at line 90, and repeatedly calls *PROCpoll* as long as *quit%* is still FALSE. Line 510 in *PROCpoll* makes the actual call to **Wimp_Poll**, returning the reason code in *reason%*. The poll loop and reason codes will be described fully in Chapter 3, but for the moment we will respond to only one reason code - code 0, which means that nothing much has happened. As soon as our program receives this code (which it is likely to do soon after initialisation), it calls *PROCerror* (see below) with an error message passed as a parameter, and also sets *quit%* to TRUE. This is picked up at the end of the loop in line 110 and so the loop is terminated, leading on to lines 120-130 which call **Wimp_CloseDown** and exit.

INTRODUCTION TO ERROR HANDLING

One fact about Wimp programming that has to be understood at an early stage is that error handling is of the utmost importance. In a multi-tasking environment it is just not acceptable for a program to crash the computer if an error occurs, since other applications may have unsaved data which would then be lost. The programmer must therefore be aware of potential errors and build in code which enables the program at best to handle the error internally with minimum fuss, or at worst to exit in a dignified fashion without disturbing other applications. For now, it is sufficient to know that a SWI call, **Wimp_ReportError**, is provided specifically to deal with errors under the Wimp. This displays a standard Wimp error box containing the text of your choice. If you are not sure what these boxes look like, the quickest way to see one is to generate an error deliberately by, for example, clicking on a disc drive icon when there is no disc in the drive.

It is normal to place a program's error reporting routine in a separate procedure, typically named *PROCerror* as we have done here, which is then called when necessary from elsewhere in the program, with a string parameter containing the text which you wish to display in the error box.

We will look at error handling and **Wimp_ReportError** in more detail in Chapter 4, but we ought to explain what is actually happening in our program. The call itself requires a pointer to a parameter block to be passed in R0, a set of flags in R1, and a task name or similar in R2 which will be used in the error box title. The block must contain a four-byte word containing the error number, followed by the text string to be displayed, terminated by a zero byte. This is set up in line 740. Don't worry too much at the moment about the error number to use - we have employed 255 here. The flags byte is a little complex and will be described in Chapter 4, but the value of 1 which we have used here means "include an OK icon". In other words, when the error box is displayed, there will be an OK icon which must be clicked on before the program can proceed. If we had used a value of 3 instead, this would display both an OK and a Cancel icon.

You will hopefully have seen by now that the code required to get a program to multi-task is quite trivial indeed. Nevertheless, we have some way to go before our program does anything useful, and in Chapter 2 we will take the next step on that road by describing how to create and open a window. Before reading further, however, you may like to take time to reflect on, and if necessary re-read this chapter, as it is important to understand fully the concepts which lie behind the use of the Wimp. It is certainly worthwhile typing in the program listed here and running it, despite its rather limited and artificial function.

2. Windows

Introduction to windows - Creating a window - Example program - Window size - Scroll offsets - Window colours - Window flags - Window title - Work area flags - Miscellaneous window information - Opening and closing a window

In Chapter 1 we saw how to initialise and close down a task, and we also introduced the Wimp poll and error handling. It's now time to start tackling the real meat of the Wimp, starting with the first letter of our acronym. We must repeat our earlier statement that although the Wimp might appear daunting at first, it is really quite straightforward once you get the hang of it, so if there is anything in this chapter that you don't understand initially, don't give up, but re-read it and experiment with the program listings until you can see exactly what is going on.

INTRODUCTION TO WINDOWS

Figure 2.1 shows a typical window as it appears on the screen, while Figure 2.2 illustrates the constituent parts of the window. It is assumed that you are familiar with the effects of clicking the mouse when the pointer is over the various parts of the window. If not, switch on your machine, read your User Guide, and find out!

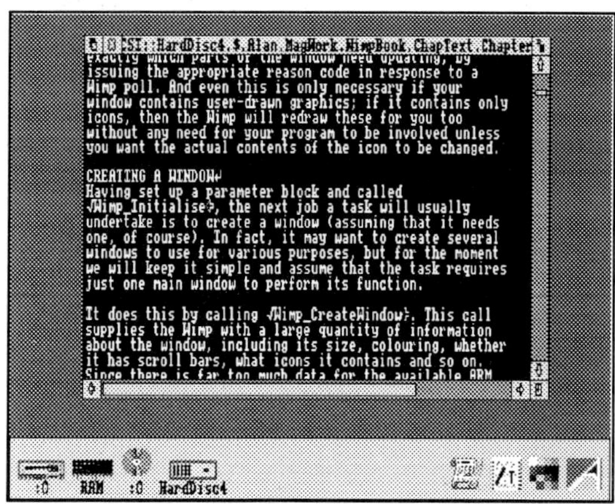

Figure 2.1
A typical window on the Desktop

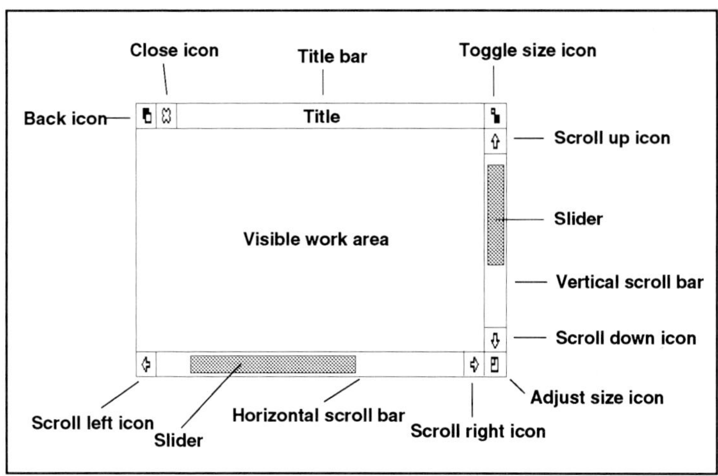

Figure 2.2
The constituent parts of a window

The really excellent thing about the Acorn Wimp is that not only will it place windows on the screen exactly where you want them, but it will fully maintain them as well. For example, if you drag a window to a new position on the screen, then the window manager will handle this for you. Only if part of the window needs redrawing (as it would if it had previously been obscured by another window) will your program need to do anything, and in such cases the Wimp will tell you exactly which parts of the window need updating, by issuing the appropriate reason code in response to a Wimp poll. And even this is only necessary if your window contains user-drawn graphics or text; if it contains only icons, then the Wimp will redraw these for you too without any need for your program to be involved unless you want the actual contents of the icon to be changed.

CREATING A WINDOW

Having set up a parameter block and called **Wimp_Initialise**, the next job a task will usually undertake is to create a window (assuming that it needs one, of course). In fact, it may want to create several windows to use for various purposes, but for the moment we will keep it simple and assume that the task requires just one main window to perform its function.

It does this by calling **Wimp_CreateWindow**. This call supplies the Wimp with a large quantity of information about the window, including its size, colouring, whether it has scroll bars, what icons it contains and so on. Since there is far too much data for the available ARM registers, the information is supplied in a parameter block, and the address of the block is itself passed as a parameter in register R1. On exit, the parameter block remains unchanged, but R0 contains the window handle. This is an identification number assigned by the Wimp to this particular window, and is unique - no two windows in existence at the same time will have the same number, whichever task they belong to. The handle must be quoted whenever a call is made subsequently to the Wimp which relates to that window. The way in which this is done is clearly detailed in the description of each call.

Offset	Contents
block+0	Visible Area minimum x co-ordinate
4	Visible Area minimum y co-ordinate
8	Visible Area maximum x co-ordinate
12	Visible Area maximum y co-ordinate
16	Scroll x offset relative to Work Area origin
20	Scroll y offset relative to Work Area origin
24	Handle to open window behind or -1=top -2=bottom
28	Window flags
32	Title foreground and frame colour (&FF=no frame)
33	Title background colour
34	Work Area foreground colour
35	Work Area background colour (&FF=transparent)
36	Scroll bar outer colour
37	Scroll bar slider colour
38	Title background colour when input focus gained
39	Reserved (must be 0)
40	Work Area minimum x co-ordinate
44	Work Area minimum y co-ordinate
48	Work Area maximum x co-ordinate
52	Work Area maximum y co-ordinate
56	Title bar icon flags
60	Work Area flags
64	Sprite area control block pointer (+1 for Wimp sprite area)
68	Minimum width of window (0 to use title width)
70	Minimum height of window
72	Title data
84	No. of icons in initial definition
88	Icon blocks (32 bytes each)

Figure 2.3
Parameter block for SWI "Wimp_CreateWindow" (&400C1)

Figure 2.3 gives the contents of the parameter block for **Wimp_CreateWindow**. This may look rather daunting at first sight, but all these parameters will be explained in the course of this chapter. By now, you are probably itching to get a window of your own on the screen, so we will leave a detailed description of **Wimp_CreateWindow** until later, and introduce Listing 2.1, which will create and open a window for you. This should be added to Listing 1.1 from the previous chapter - in other words, you will be updating the *!RunImage* program for the *OurTask* application which you should have already created.

Don't worry if there is anything in the listing you don't understand - all will be revealed in due course. You will notice that the listing uses three further SWI calls which have not been mentioned so far - **Wimp_OpenWindow**, **Wimp_CloseWindow** and **Wimp_GetWindowState**. These will also be described fully later.

In this and most subsequent updates to the program, some of the new lines will replace existing lines of the same number. Where a blank line is shown, this means that the existing line of that number must be deleted.

When run, the program places a window on the screen, as illustrated in Figure 2.4. This can be dragged, scrolled or re-sized as required but performs no other function. When you click on the Close icon, the window will close and the task will terminate. We have kept things simple for the moment in order to illustrate only those concepts which are relevant to this chapter.

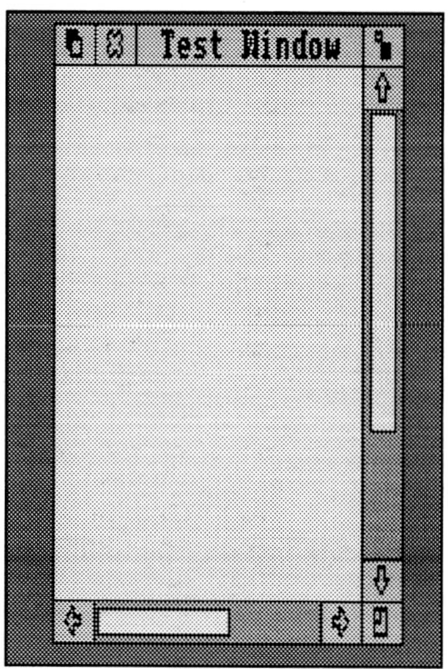

Figure 2.4
Window created by Listing 2.1

Unfortunately it is necessary for *OurTask* to respond to **Wimp_Poll** reason codes before we are able to explain them fully. This is unavoidable since no Wimp program can work without calling **Wimp_Poll**. The polling routines will be fully covered in the next chapter. For now, you will just have to take it on trust that the routine at lines 500-680 does actually work.

Listing 2.1

```
   30 REM Updated to Chapter 2
  190 ON ERROR PROCerror(REPORT$+" at line "+STR$ERL):
SYS "Wimp_CloseDown":END
  200 whandle%=FNcreate_window(200,200,300,500,200,200
)
  440 !block%=whandle%
  450 SYS "Wimp_GetWindowState",,block%
  460 SYS "Wimp_OpenWindow",,block%
  530
  540
  550 WHEN 2:SYS "Wimp_OpenWindow",,block%
  560 WHEN 3:SYS "Wimp_CloseWindow",,block%
  570 quit%=TRUE
 1000 DEF FNcreate_window(x%,y%,w%,h%,extx%,exty%)
 1010 :
 1020 REM visible work area
 1030 !block%=x%
 1040 block%!4=y%
 1050 block%!8=x%+w%
 1060 block%!12=y%+h%
 1070 :
 1080 REM scroll offsets
 1090 block%!16=0
 1100 block%!20=0
 1110 :
 1120 REM handle behind and window flags
 1130 block%!24=-1
 1140 block%!28=&FF000012
 1150 :
 1160 REM window colours
 1170 block%?32=7
 1180 block%?33=2
 1190 block%?34=7
 1200 block%?35=1
 1210 block%?36=3
 1220 block%?37=1
 1230 block%?38=12
 1240 :
 1250 REM work area extent
```

```
1260 block%!40=0
1270 block%!44=-h%-exty%
1280 block%!48=w%+extx%
1290 block%!52=0
1300 :
1310 REM title bar and work area flags
1320 block%!56=&19
1330 block%!60=3<<12
1340 :
1350 REM sprite area pointer and minimum size
1360 block%!64=0
1370 block%!68=0
1380 :
1390 REM window title
1400 $(block%+72)="Test Window"
1410 :
1420 REM number of icons
1430 block%!84=0
1440 :
1450 SYS "Wimp_CreateWindow",,block% TO handle%
1460 =handle%
1470 :
```

PROGRAM DESCRIPTION

We will now describe in detail the calls which have been used, starting with **Wimp_CreateWindow**. The information supplied with this call can be broken down into several sections: window size, scroll offsets, window colours, window flags and title bar information, plus one or two miscellaneous pieces of data. In the program, the function *FNcreate_window* is used to place all this information into the parameter block and to create the window. Line 200 calls *FNcreate_window* and places the returned value in the variable *whandle%* (this will be the window handle). Six parameters must be supplied to the function, all of which relate to the window size, as we shall see in just a moment.

Lines 1020-1430 of the function are concerned purely and simply with setting up the parameter block, and will be described in detail below. To see how this works you will need to be familiar with the ?, ! and $ indirection operators. These are described in Appendix A. Finally, lines 1450-1460 make the call to **Wimp_CreateWindow** and return the window handle.

WINDOW SIZE

The first two parameters to *FNcreate_window* (*x%* and *y%*) are the x and y co-ordinates of the bottom left-hand corner of the visible part of the window (relative to the graphics origin which is at the bottom left of the screen). The next two (*w%* and *h%*) are the width and height of the visible part of the window. All these values are quoted in standard OS graphics units (i.e. the same units which are used for PLOT commands and so on). It is not necessary for all of the window to be visible on the screen, and so the last two parameters to the function determine the extent of the window, i.e. the size of the hidden parts, which will only appear if the window is scrolled or extended in size. *extx%* and *exty%* therefore represent the amount by which the total extent of the window exceeds the visible part in the horizontal and vertical directions respectively. The visible part of the window is known as the *visible area,* and the total extent of the window, including the hidden parts, is known as the *work area* - see Figure 2.5.

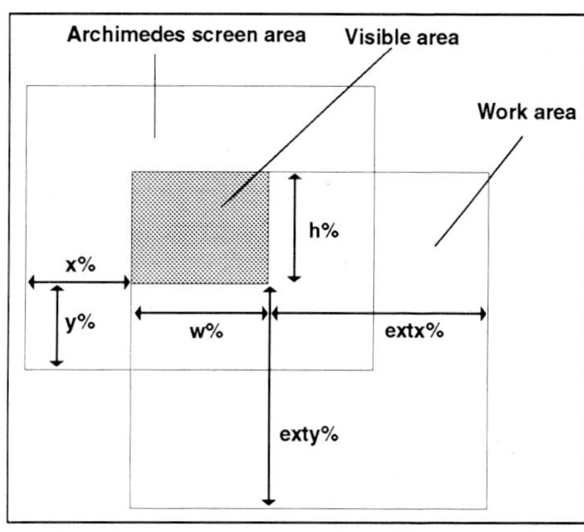

Figure 2.5
Simplified relationship between the visible area and the work area

Lines 1030-1060 place the four co-ordinates of the visible part of the window (left x, bottom y, right x, and top y respectively) into the block. Lines 1260-1290 do the same for the co-ordinates of the entire extent of the window - the work area.

In fact, although the visible area is measured in standard graphics units from the bottom left-hand corner of the screen, the work area co-ordinates must be given relative to the top left-hand corner of the visible area. If you look closely at lines 1260-1290 you can see how this works in practice. Because we want the visible area and the work area to coincide at the top left-hand corner, the left x and top y co-ordinates of the work area will be the same as those of the visible area. Relative to the visible area, then, they are zero, and this is the value we have used (in block+40 and block+52). The right x and bottom y co-ordinates of the work area, however, will extend from the top left-hand corner of the visible area for a distance of *w%+extx%* and *h%+exty%* respectively. In the case of the y co-ordinates, the values must be negative, since y values start at the bottom of the screen and increase upwards. So if you look at the relevant lines in the listing:

```
1270 block%!44=-h%-exty%
1280 block%!48=w%+extx%
```

you should be able to see how this works.

Don't worry too much about all this at the moment - for many simple Wimp programs the relationship between the two sets of co-ordinates is irrelevant since the work area and the visible area will be the same. Furthermore, once the screen co-ordinates of the window have been entered into the parameter block at the time of creation, many tasks have no further need to worry about co-ordinates at all. Even this initial process can often be done by trial and error - simply experiment with the co-ordinates you supply in the block until the window appears to be the right size and shape and in the right place. And as we shall see later in the book, there is an application available from Acorn which takes all the hard work out of designing windows.

For the moment at least, we will deal simply in terms of the six parameters supplied to the function *FNcreate_window*. To reiterate, these are the x and y co-ordinates of the bottom left-hand corner of the visible area, and its width and height, and the additional width and height of the non-visible part of the window (both of which could be zero, but in our example are not). We have given scroll offsets of zero in our listing for the moment - this means that the visible area will be at the top left of the work area. We will examine the subject of scroll offsets shortly, but first you may like to experiment with the figures supplied to *FNcreate_window* in line 200 to see the way in which the various parameters relate to one another, and how altering one or more of the figures will change the shape and/or size of the window displayed on the screen. For example, you could try the following modifications, and see the effect these have on the size and shape of the window, and on the scroll bars:

```
200 whandle%=FNcreate_window(200,200,800,200,0,0)
```

or:

```
200 whandle%=FNcreate_window(0,1024,600,600,10000,100
00)
```

MINIMUM WINDOW SIZE

By dragging the Adjust Size icon at the bottom right-hand corner of a scrollable window the user can adjust the size of the visible area. The minimum size possible is taken from the two 16-bit parameters at block+68 and block+70. If these are set to zero (as they are in line 1370 in Listing 2.1), the minimum width is taken to be the width of the window's title string, while the minimum height is the vertical space necessary for any scroll bars and arrows. You can verify this by dragging the Adjust Size icon on the test program. Try also supplying different minima. A line similar to the following will do the trick:

```
1370 block%!68=300+400<<16
```

This line will place the value 300 at block+68, and 400 at block+70 - the "<<16" at the end means shift the second value to the left by 16 bits. This is necessary since although BBC Basic (as used on the Archimedes) has single-byte and four-byte indirection operators ("?" and "!"), it has no double-byte equivalent.

SCROLL OFFSETS

At block+16 and block+20 of the parameter block, the x and y scroll offsets must be supplied. These are 32-bit words giving the initial relationship between the visible area and the work area; in other words the scroll offsets determine which part of the total work area of the window is currently visible. You can see this concept in operation each time you scroll a window on the Desktop by clicking on the scroll arrow icons - as the scroll bar (and hence the window's scroll offset) moves, the visible area changes. The two offsets are usefully defined as the co-ordinates in the work area of that pixel which is displayed at the top left-hand corner of the visible area.

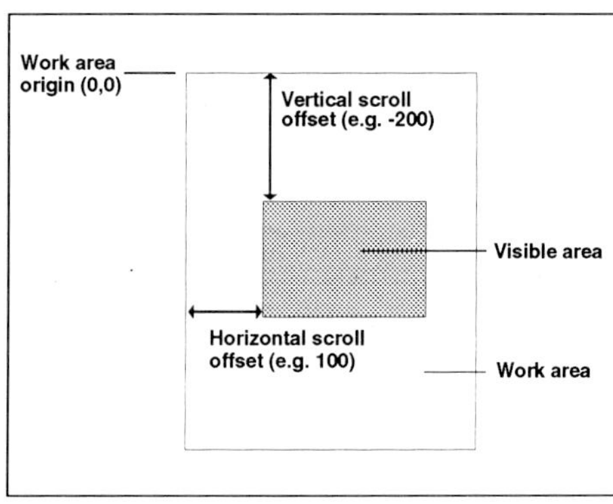

Figure 2.6
Applying scroll offsets

In Listing 2.1, these two offsets are left as zero (lines 1090-1100). This results in the top left-hand corner of the visible area coinciding with the origin of the work area, i.e. the top left-hand corner. When you run the program you will see this confirmed by the position of the scroll bars. The horizontal one is at the extreme left, and the vertical one at the top of its range.

Since the work area of our

window is larger than the visible area, we could if we wanted supply horizontal and/or vertical scroll offsets in the parameter block. The x offset must be positive, since you can only ever scroll to the right of the work area origin, while the y offset must be negative, since you can only ever scroll below the origin.

Thus if we were to supply a horizontal scroll offset of 100 (at block+16), then the left-hand edge of the visible area would be 100 graphics units from the left-hand edge of the work area (see Figure 2.6). Similarly, if we set the vertical scroll offset (at block+20) to -200, the top of the visible area will be 200 units below the top of the work area. The values 100 and -200 are of course just the starting values of the two scroll offsets. Both may be adjusted to any value using the scroll bars. To experiment with this, you could change lines 1090-1100 as follows:

```
1090 block%!16=100
1100 block%!20=-200
```

These modifications to the program will produce initial scroll offsets as described above.

WINDOW COLOURS

Lines 1170-1230 establish the colours of the various parts of the window, which are stored from block+32 to block+38. The values supplied are single-byte, and correspond to the standard Wimp palette (see Figure 2.7). Generally speaking it is desirable to adhere to the colour numbers we have used in *OurTask*, as these have been chosen to conform with Acorn's own guidelines about the appearance and functionality of Wimp programs.

0-7	Linear grey scale (white=0, black=7)
8	Dark blue
9	Yellow
10	Light green
11	Red
12	Cream
13	Dark green
14	Orange
15	Light blue

Figure 2.7
16-colour Wimp palette

Acorn is very keen that programmers should stick to these guidelines to achieve conformity within the Desktop, and to present the user with an interface which is intuitive to use and does not require common processes to be re-learned each time a new package is encountered. However, in order to gain an insight into the way the window parameters are set up, you might like to experiment a little with different colours, just to prove that this is not all fiction. For a really garish window, for example, you could try altering some of the lines as follows:

```
1170 block%?32=11
1180 block%?33=10
1200 block%?35=14
1210 block%?36=7
1220 block%?37=15
```

WINDOW FLAGS

Three of the 32-bit word parameters passed to **Wimp_CreateWindow** contain sets of flags which determine the properties of the window created. A flag may be considered as a variable which has just two possible values. For example, the flag which determines whether the window has vertical scroll bars or not can obviously only take one of two values. Wimp flags are each represented by a single bit of a given 32-bit parameter word - each bit taking the value 1 (set) or 0 (unset). Bit 0 is the least significant bit of the word, while bit 31 is the most significant.

The most complex of these sets of flags is the Window Flags group, situated at block+28. Figure 2.8 shows the function of each. As is the case with so many aspects of the Wimp, there is a lot of detail to be mastered, but much of it will lose its mystique as you experiment and see exactly how it all relates to the visual appearance of the window.

In the *OurTask* program, the window flags are supplied as a single 32-bit hex value (line 1140), which in this case is &FF000012 (it is normal practice to supply the figure in hex in this way). Because it is tedious to calculate such values for each window that you generate, and because the use of a separate variable for each flag would be cumbersome, Listing 2.2 at the end of this chapter is provided as a shortcut. When you run this program it takes you through all the features covered by the window flags, requesting a yes/no response for each. At the end it prints out a single 32-bit hex value for the window flags, to be used at block+28 when you are creating the window. The value obtained may be substituted at line 1140 of Listing 2.1. The meaning of each flag is largely self-explanatory, but one or two are more obscure, and some further explanation is necessary.

0	Unused
1	Window can be dragged
2	Unused
3	Unused
4	Wimp can redraw window on its own without help from task (i.e. no user graphics)
5	Window is a pane (on a tool window)
6	Window can extend outside screen area
7	Unused
8	Generate scroll request events
9	As 8 but no auto repeat on arrow icons
10	Treat window colours as GCOL rather than Wimp colours
11	Don't allow windows below this one
12	Generate key-pressed reason codes for hot keys
13-15	Reserved - must be zero
16-20	Used to return info only
21-23	Reserved - must be zero
24	Window has a Back icon
25	Window has a Close icon
26	Window has a title bar
27	Window has a Toggle Size icon
28	Window has a vertical scroll bar
29	Window has an Adjust Size icon
30	Window has a horizontal scroll bar
31	Must be set (i.e. 1)

Figure 2.8
Window flags (at block%+28)
(flags marked "unused" were used in an earlier version of the window manager, and are now obsolete)

Flag 4 should only be set if the window *does not* contain elements such as graphics which the Wimp cannot update automatically when redrawing the window. In other words, set this bit if the Wimp needs no help from the task in redrawing the window. Our window does not yet contain any graphics, so this bit must be set for the moment in our program.

Flag 5 is only set if the window is a very special kind - a so-called pane like the toolbox window attached to the left-hand edge of a Draw window. For most purposes it is not necessary to worry about this bit, and in our program we have left it unset.

Flags 8 and 9 are only set if the task needs to know when the user has performed a scroll request (e.g. by clicking on a scroll arrow icon or dragging a scroll bar). For most purposes it is unnecessary to set these bits since the Wimp will handle the process of scrolling the window on its own if they are unset, but occasionally a task may want to know that a scroll has been requested so that it can perform some action (perhaps to increment a line count to show the position in a document), or it may want to set the new scroll offset to a value determined by the task itself. As an example, a text editor may want to ensure that the top or bottom of the visible area always coincides with the start of a line of text - Edit does this when you scroll up and down through a document, for example.

Flag 10 determines how colour is handled. There are two possible palettes that a window can use, the ordinary GCOL palette allowing up to 255 colours (i.e. colours 0-254; 255 cannot be used because the value 255 is used as a flag), or the more restricted Wimp palette. Unless there are compelling reasons to do otherwise, you should keep to the Wimp palette. Flag 10 is set if you are using GCOL colours.

Flag 12 is known as the "hot keys" flag. It is only set if the task wishes to be notified when the user presses a key which is not subsequently claimed by any other task. Normally, all key presses are sent first to the task which currently owns the caret. If that task does not wish to process that particular key, it is then passed in turn to any other tasks which have windows open with the hot keys flag set. This facility is often used to implement functions which can be accessed at any time with a single key press, irrespective of the position of the caret or the pointer (for example to dump the current screen to disc as a sprite, or to open a commonly-used directory on a disc). This is known as a "hot keys" facility; hence the name of the flag. An obvious example is the use of function key F12 by the Task Manager to access the command line. For the moment, our program will not make use of the hot keys facility.

The only flags which are worth experimenting with at this stage are 1, 6 and 24-30. Try a value of &FF000010 (i.e. bit 1 unset) and see what happens when you try to drag the window. Then try &FF000052 (bit 6 set) and see what happens when you drag the window to the edge of the screen. Other flag settings you could try are &8F000012, &D6000012 or &80000010. See if you can work out why they have the effect they do, but be warned - if you use the last of these (&80000010) you will need to reset the computer with Ctrl-Break in order to quit the application and remove the window from the screen. It should not be too difficult to see why this is so.

WINDOW TITLE

The title of the window may be displayed in the standard system font or in anti-aliased text, or it may even be a sprite. In any case it must fit between the horizontal bounding lines of the title bar at the top of the window. The Title Bar Flags, which define the nature of the title, are placed as a 32-bit value in the parameter block at block+56, and the details of the text (or of the sprite) are passed at block+72 upwards. We will start by looking at the flags, but to keep things simple we will only list those which you are likely to use when setting up short text-based titles in the system font (see Figure 2.9), since it is quite rare for window title bars to use either sprites or anti-aliased text (the latter requires a much longer time to be redrawn and therefore slows down the process of updating windows quite considerably).

0	Icon contains text
3	Contents are centred horizontally
4	Contents are centred vertically
9	Text is right justified

Figure 2.9
Selected title bar flags

For a simple text title, there is very little work to do. To give horizontally and vertically centred system font text the flag should have a binary value of 11001 (&19 hex). As for the title string itself, in its simplest form, which we shall use here, it is placed as a text string at block+72 onwards. Using this method, it must be of no more than 12 characters, and must be terminated by the addition of a control character (e.g. ASCII 0 or ASCII 13) if it is less than 12 characters in length. This is achieved in line 1400 of Listing 2.1:

```
1400 $(block%+72)="Test Window"
```

The control character ASCII 13 is automatically placed at the end of the string by the $ operator.

WORK AREA FLAGS

The final set of flags used by **Wimp_CreateWindow** are the Work Area Flags. These are concerned solely with the response of the Wimp to the mouse. Although the whole of the 32-bit word at block+60 is set aside for this purpose, only bits 12-15 are used. Figure 2.10 gives the possible values which these four bits may take. It is important to note that in contrast to the other sets of flags the 4 bits here are treated as a single 4-bit word which can take one of 16 unique and mutually exclusive values (i.e. any integer in the range 0-15).

0	Ignore all clicks
1	Notify task continually while pointer is over work area
2	Click notifies task (auto-repeat)
3	Click notifies task (once only)
4	Release over work area notifies task
5	Double-click notifies task
6	As 3 but can also drag (returns button state*16)
7	As 4 but can also drag (returns button state*16)
8	As 5 but can also drag (returns button state*16)
9	As 3
10	Click returns button state*256 Drag returns button state*16 Double-click returns button state*1
11	Click returns button state Drag returns button state*16
12-14	Reserved
15	Mouse clicks cause window to gain input focus (e.g. for text entry)

Figure 2.10
Work Area Flags (integer values)

The term "button state" indicates which of the mouse buttons is being used to generate the click when it is reported to the task. A different value is returned for each button, and this can be used by the task to determine whether the user wishes to open a menu, activate a process or whatever, in accordance with the standard conventions for using each of the three buttons.

Because we are putting a 4-bit integer value into this flag word starting at bit 12, we must shift the value 12 bits to the left. This is done by using the shift operator that we met earlier:

```
block%!60=val%<<12
```

where *val%* is the integer value taken from the list in Figure 2.10. In Listing 2.1 we have used a value of 3 (i.e. Click notifies task), and so we have stored 3<<12 (i.e. &3000) at block+60 in line 1330. The exact value chosen for the task will appear more relevant when we begin to look at **Wimp_Poll** in the next chapter. This is because the setting of the work area flags will determine how the Wimp responds to our poll requests.

MISCELLANEOUS WINDOW INFORMATION

There are still a few loose ends to be tied up in our description of the window parameter block. You will see in Listing 2.1 that line 1130 supplies a parameter entitled "handle behind". This tells the Wimp where in the stack of windows visible on the screen we want ours to appear. A specific window handle can be supplied, in which case ours will be opened immediately behind it, or we can supply a value of -1 (top of stack) or -2 (bottom of stack). Normally we want our window to be opened on top of any which are already there, so it is usual to supply a value of -1, as here.

At block+64 (line 1360) we can insert a pointer to a sprite area, in case our window or its icons use sprites. We will look at this further when we deal with icons, but for the moment we can leave this value as zero.

Finally, at block+84 (line 1430) we must insert the number of icons which are being defined within the window block (the icon definitions if present start at block+88 and require 32 bytes each). We have not concerned ourselves with icons yet, and so this value can also be left as zero for now.

OPENING A WINDOW

In case you're tempted to imagine that all this elaborate complexity we have just described will now put a window on the screen, it won't! It merely defines the window for subsequent use, and in order to open it we must make a further call to the Wimp, which is **Wimp_OpenWindow**. This also requires a parameter block, the details of which are shown in Figure 2.11. You will see that each time the window is opened (which may be at the explicit command of the program or it may be in response to a request from the Wimp when the user has dragged or re-sized the window), the co-ordinates, scroll offsets and window flags must again be specified.

block+0	Window handle
4	Visible Area minimum x co-ordinate
8	Visible Area minimum y co-ordinate
12	Visible Area maximum x co-ordinate
16	Visible Area maximum y co-ordinate
20	Scroll x offset relative to Work Area origin
24	Scroll y offset relative to Work Area origin
28	Handle to open window behind (or -1 if top of stack, -2 if bottom)
32	Window flags

Figure 2.11
Parameter block for SWI "Wimp_OpenWindow" (&400C5)

Before you throw up your hands in horror, however, things are not as black as they look. Fortunately there is in either case a shortcut which avoids the need to calculate all these values yet again. In the case of requests from the Wimp, the block is actually set up for you, so all you have to do is call **Wimp_OpenWindow** safe in the knowledge that all the information is already there (as in line 550). In cases where you want to open the window yourself (for example when the program is first run), there is another call, **Wimp_GetWindowState** (&400CB), which can obtain the values for you. This call returns the parameter block you need for **Wimp_OpenWindow**, containing the values which were current last time the window was opened or created.

You can see all this in action in Listing 2.1. Once the window has been created, lines 450-460 call **Wimp_GetWindowState** followed by **Wimp_OpenWindow**. This places the window on the screen at the co-ordinates which were specified when the window was created. As an experiment, try removing line 450 and see what happens when you run the program - you will most likely get a funny-shaped window which looks nothing like the one you expected.

Subsequent openings of the window are done in line 550 in response to a request from the Wimp, and here the call is made without any further ado since the correct data is already in the block.

CLOSING A WINDOW

One further call needs to be considered in this chapter: **Wimp_CloseWindow** (&400C6). As you might expect, you should make this call whenever you wish to close a window. Often this will be a response to the Wimp after the user has clicked on the window's Close icon. The only parameter required is the window handle in block+0, and the block address is passed in R1 as usual. If the call is made in response to a request from the Wimp then the window handle will already be in the correct position in the block. In Listing 2.1 we have arranged for the task to terminate if the window is closed (by setting *quit%* to TRUE in line 570). Strictly speaking it is not necessary to close windows before terminating a task, since the Wimp will automatically close any open windows in these circumstances, but we have done so here to illustrate the use of the call.

We have covered a lot of ground in this chapter, and if your head is still reeling from all this complex information, do please re-read any sections which are unclear, and experiment with the program until you can see what is happening. In the next chapter we will look at **Wimp_Poll** in detail.

Listing 2.2

```
   10 REM >Flagset
   20 REM by Lee Calcraft
   30 REM Generates window flag values
   40 :
   50 MODE 12
   60 flag%=1<<31:REM set top bit
   70 PRINT"WIMP WINDOW FLAG GENERATOR"
   80 PRINT'"Generates 32-bit window flag for use with
 Wimp_CreateWindow"
   90 PRINT'"Respond with Y (=YES) or any other key (=N
 O)"
  100 PRINT"to questions below about the window you are
 creating"'
  110 REPEAT
  120 READ A%,A$
  130 IF A%<255 THEN
  140 PRINTA$;" (bit ";A%;")";TAB(44)"Y/N ? ";
  150 B%=GET AND &DF
  160 B%=-(B%=ASC"Y")
  170 IF B% THEN PRINT"Y" ELSE PRINT"N"
  180 flag%+=B%<<A%
  190 ENDIF
  200 UNTIL A%=255
  210 PRINT'"Window flag= &";~flag%
  220 END
  230 :
  240 DATA 1,Draggable,4,Can be updated entirely by Wim
 p
  250 DATA 5,Pane,6,Extend beyond screen
  260 DATA 8,Scroll event (with auto rpt)
  270 DATA 9,Scroll event (with no repeat)
  280 DATA 10,GCOL (=not Wimp colours)
  290 DATA 11,Windows below prohibited
  300 DATA 12,Hot key events
  310 DATA 24,Back icon,25,Close icon
  320 DATA 26,Title bar,27,Toggle size
  330 DATA 28,Vertical scroll,30,Horizontal scroll
  340 DATA 29,Adjust size icon,255,
```

3. The Wimp Poll

The poll loop - Example program - Null reason codes - Requests to open or close a window - Pointer over window - Mouse clicks - Key presses - Masking events

THE POLL LOOP

The Wimp poll loop is central to the operation of any Wimp task, and is the means by which the task responds to external events, such as a click of the mouse, a character typed at the keyboard, or even just the fact that the pointer has moved over one of the task's windows. If you look back at Listing 2.1 in the last chapter you will see that the procedure in *OurTask* which deals with this vital operation is *PROCpoll* (lines 500-680). These lines as they stand at present are repeated in Figure 3.1.

```
500 DEF PROCpoll
510 SYS "Wimp_Poll",0,block% TO reason%
520 CASE reason% OF
550 WHEN 2:SYS "Wimp_OpenWindow",,block%
560 WHEN 3:SYS "Wimp_CloseWindow",,block%
570 quit%=TRUE
670 ENDCASE
680 ENDPROC
```

Figure 3.1
The Wimp poll loop from Chapter 2

While any task is operative, a segment of code of this kind must be repeatedly called. In due course the Wimp will return a so-called *reason code* to the task (in our program it is returned to the variable *reason%*), and the CASE statement in the procedure responds to this in various ways. So far our program has only responded to reason codes 2 and 3, but the full range of codes is currently from 0-19 and these are shown in Figure 3.2 (RISC OS 3 recognises an additional reason code, number 13, but we will not be using this in our demonstration listings). As soon as it has responded, the program calls *PROCpoll* (and hence **Wimp_Poll**) again, and waits for a new reason code to come back.

Code	Event
0	Null_Reason_Code
1	Redraw_Window_Request
2	Open_Window_Request
3	Close_Window_Request
4	Pointer_Leaving_Window
5	Pointer_Entering_Window
6	Mouse_Click
7	User_Drag_Box
8	Key_pressed
9	Menu_Selection
10	Scroll_Request
11	Lose_Caret
12	Gain_Caret
13	PollWord_NonZero (RISC OS 3 only)
14-16	Reserved
17	User_Message
18	User_Message_Recorded
19	User_Message_Acknowledge

Figure 3.2
Reason codes returned by SWI "Wimp_Poll" (&400C7)

In the time between receiving the poll request from our task, and returning a reason code to it, the Wimp will service each of the other active tasks in turn. In this way the Wimp performs what is known as *co-operative multi-tasking*. It is called co-operative since it relies on each task being well behaved, and not delaying too long between receiving a reason code and re-polling the Wimp (there is another kind of multi-tasking which is implemented on some other computer systems called *pre-emptive multi-tasking*, in which each task is allocated a strict time slice in rotation).

The most widely used reason codes are those from 0-3, 6-9 and 17-19, though many applications may need to respond to some or all of the others. Listing 3.1 given below is intended to be added to the *OurTask* program, which then provides a set of routines to respond to reason codes 0, 2-6 and 8. Some of the other reason codes will be introduced in later chapters as appropriate. In all cases except code 0, the Wimp returns relevant information in the parameter block.

Listing 3.1

```
  30 REM Updated to Chapter 3
 165 count%=0
 530 WHEN 0:VDU4:PRINTTAB(0,0)count%:VDU5:count%+=1
 580 WHEN 4:SOUND 1,-10,80,4
 590 WHEN 5:SOUND 1,-10,200,4
 600 WHEN 6:PROCclick(block%!8)
 620 WHEN 8:PROCkeypress(block%!24)
1140 block%!28=&FF001012
1500 DEF PROCclick(button%)
1510 CASE button% OF
1520 WHEN 1:a$="Adjust"
1530 WHEN 2:a$="Menu"
1540 WHEN 4:a$="Select"
1550 ENDCASE
1560 PROCerror("You have clicked the "+a$+" button")
1680 ENDPROC
1690 :
1700 DEF PROCkeypress(key%)
1710 CASE TRUE OF
1720 WHEN key%<>&1CC
1730 PROCerror("You have pressed a key - ASCII code "
+STR$key%+" (hex &"+STR$~key%+")")
1740 OTHERWISE:SYS "Wimp_ProcessKey",key%
1750 ENDCASE
1880 ENDPROC
1890 :
```

POLL REASON CODES IN DETAIL

You will notice that the CASE statement in the poll loop has now been enlarged to take account of the additional reason codes to which we want to respond. We will now describe in turn each of the reason codes recognised by *OurTask*. You may find it instructive before reading any further to try to work out for yourself what the program will do, by referring to Figure 3.2 and matching the reason codes listed there with the WHEN statements in the poll loop. If you have typed the program in, you can try out your theories by performing various actions and seeing whether the results are what you expect.

NULL CODES

For most of the time the reason code returned by the Wimp will be zero, indicating that nothing is happening that requires any action from the task. You may be wondering why the task ever needs to receive this null reason code; after all, we said earlier that the Wimp only troubles your task when some processing is required in response to an external action by the user. But there are some applications which may want to perform background activities, such as printing a document or updating a clock for example. It would be inconvenient to expect the user to click continually with the mouse to communicate with the task and keep the background operation going, and so these applications will make use of the null reason code to perform a small part of the operation before passing control back to the Wimp. In other words, they are saying to the Wimp "Tell me when nothing is happening and I can do a bit of my work in the slack period". Tasks which do not need to act on null reason codes can tell the Wimp not to bother to report them, as we will see shortly.

OurTask responds to null reason codes in line 530. This simply prints an incremented value (held in *count%*) in the top left-hand corner of the screen each time the program receives a null code. When you run the program, you will see the value displayed on the screen increasing all the time as long as there is nothing much else happening. You should note that Wimp tasks do not normally write directly to the screen like this; after all, the whole point of a multi-tasking Wimp environment is that each task should restrict its display to its own windows. We have done it here only because it is a simple way to illustrate a response to null reason codes, and we shall remove this section of code in the next chapter. In the meantime, don't take this as an indication of how to display information in a window - we will show you how to do this later.

REQUESTS TO OPEN OR CLOSE A WINDOW

When you drag a window around the screen, or scroll or re-size it, reason code 2 will be returned by the Wimp (a window needs opening or re-opening). Our program responds to this in line 550 by calling **Wimp_OpenWindow**. As we saw in the previous chapter, the Wimp returns a parameter block giving the parameters of the window to be re-opened. If you omit line 550 you will find that the window will not move when you try to drag it around.

If the window operation results in no new part of the window being revealed, then the Wimp re-opens the window on its own. If on the other hand it causes a previously obscured part of the window to be uncovered, the Wimp then looks at window flag 4. If this is set (meaning that no help from the task is necessary), the Wimp goes ahead and updates the window and any icons that need redrawing. If, however, the flag is unset (meaning that the window contains text or graphics which the Wimp cannot generate without help from the application), then the Wimp will next return reason code 1 (redraw window request). The task must respond to this immediately by redrawing the window, but it needs to do this in a special way, which will be covered in detail in Chapter 7. *OurTask* has for the moment set flag 4 (in line 1140 when the window was created), and so the program does not need to respond to reason code 1 since this will never be returned.

Reason code 3 (request to close window) is returned if the user clicks on a window's Close icon. The only information needed in this case is the window handle, which is returned in block+0 ready for the task to call **Wimp_CloseWindow**.

POINTER OVER WINDOW

When you move the pointer into a window which belongs to our task, reason code 5 is generated (pointer entering window). If the pointer leaves the window, then reason code 4 is returned (pointer leaving window). These two codes return simply the window handle in block+0, and *OurTask* deals with them in lines 580 and 590. When the pointer enters the window a high-pitched sound is generated, followed by a low-pitched sound when the pointer leaves the window. Since our task only has one window, we do not need to check the returned window handle since there is only one possibility. If we had more than one window, however, we might need to add code to read the handle from the block and perform the necessary actions according to the result.

Many tasks have no need to respond to these two reason codes, since the Wimp will always tell you anyway which window and/or icon is involved when it reports a click or a keypress. But sometimes an application may want to know exactly when the pointer is over its window, perhaps to change the pointer shape, or to calculate its co-ordinates.

MOUSE CLICKS

If you click the mouse when the pointer is over the visible area of your window, reason code 6 is returned, together with a block of information which is detailed in Figure 3.3. Note that details of the pointer co-ordinates and button state are included, and we use these values rather than employing the Basic MOUSE function.

block+0	Mouse x co-ordinate
4	Mouse y co-ordinate
8	Button state
12	Window handle (or -1 for background -2 for icon bar)
16	icon handle (or -1 for work area background)

Figure 3.3
Information block returned by reason code 6 (Mouse_Click)

The mouse x and y co-ordinates (if we need them) are given as absolute screen co-ordinates rather than relative to the task window (i.e. with the origin at the bottom left-hand corner of the screen). The value for the mouse button state at block+8 will depend to a certain extent on the window's work area flags. Generally speaking the value will be 1 for a click with Adjust, 2 for a click with Menu, and 4 for a click with Select. However, as you may remember from our discussion of the work area flags in Chapter 2, it is possible to set the work area button type such that drags and/or double-clicks are also reported.

For example, if you have set the button type to 6, then if Select is clicked in the window and held down long enough to start a drag, the button value returned will be 64 (if you can't see why this should be, re-read this paragraph carefully and study Figure 2.10 in the last chapter). You will remember that OurTask set the work area flag to 3: *Click notifies task (once only).* The task will therefore be informed each time the mouse is clicked within the window, but with no auto-repeat action. The values returned at block+8 will therefore be 1, 2 or 4 as described above.

You will see that the Wimp also returns the window handle (at block+12). This is vital if a task is using more than one window, since it will need to know which of its windows is involved with the event. If the window contains icons, it is also quite likely that you will need to know which icon was under the pointer at the time of the click, and this information is also returned at block+16. We will be covering icons in detail in Chapter 5, and we will have more to say about responding to clicks over them in that chapter.

When you click with the mouse over *OurTask*'s window, an error box will be displayed telling you which button has been used. *PROCclick* in lines 1500-1680 performs this action. Strictly speaking this is not an error, of course, but we have used this method here as a simple means of displaying a message on the screen without a lot of additional code.

KEY PRESSES

The only other reason code that we shall deal with at present is code 8 (a key has been pressed). Your task will only receive this code if one of your windows either currently owns the caret or has had its hot keys flag set. The caret is the vertical cursor which appears in writable icons and editor windows to mark the current typing position. Again, a block of information is returned, as shown in Figure 3.4. *OurTask* has no provision for handling the caret at present, and so we must set the hot keys bit in order to demonstrate the use of reason code 8. To do this we need to alter the value at line 1140, and Listing 3.1 when added to the earlier listing will do this automatically. *PROCkeypress* handles the program's response to key presses, generating an error box showing the ASCII value of the key pressed.

block+0	window handle with input focus
4	Icon handle (-1 if none)
8	x-offset of caret (relative to window origin)
12	y-offset of caret (relative to window origin)
16	caret height and flags
20	index of caret into string
24	character code of key pressed (4-byte word)

Figure 3.4
Information block returned by reason code 8
(Key_Pressed)

The information at block+8, 12, 16 & 20 enables the application to work out exactly where the caret was when the key was pressed, but we don't need to worry about the details of this at this stage. However, there *are* three important things you need to note when responding to this reason code. Firstly, if the caret is visible on the Desktop (for example in a writable icon or an Edit window), key presses will be offered first to the application which owns the caret. This means that *OurTask* may not get a chance to respond to them at all.

Secondly, because the Archimedes uses a full character set, including characters 128-255 (the so-called "top bit set" characters), the Wimp cannot return function keys and other special keys as single-byte values for the obvious reason of potential ambiguity. Instead it returns them as double-byte values with the high byte set to 1 (i.e. hexadecimal values above &100). Figure 3.5 shows the values which are returned by the special keys.

Key	Alone	+Shift	+Ctrl	+Shift-Ctrl
Escape	&1B	&1B	&1B	&1B
Print (F0)	&180	&190	&1A0	&1B0
F1-F9	&181-189	&191-199	&1A1-1A9	&1B1-1B9
Tab	&18A	&19A	&1AA	&1BA
Copy	&18B	&19B	&1AB	&1BB
Left arrow	&18C	&19C	&1AC	&1BC
Right arrow	&18D	&19D	&1AD	&1BD
Down arrow	&18E	&19E	&1AE	&1BE
Up arrow	&18F	&19F	&1AF	&1BF
Page Down	&19E	&18E	&1BE	&1AE
Page Up	&19F	&18F	&1BF	&1AF
F10-F12	&1CA-1CC	&1DA-1DC	&1EA-1EC	&1FA-1FC
Insert	&1CD	&1DD	&1ED	&1FD

Figure 3.5
Values returned by the Wimp for special keys

Thirdly, note line 1740 which makes a call to another SWI, **Wimp_ProcessKey** (&400DC). Any application which responds to reason code 8 *must* make this call if it receives a key press which it does not recognise or does not wish to process. The SWI takes just one parameter in R0, which is the ASCII code of the key. This must be done so that other applications can be given the chance to act on the information. As a clear example of this, you will be aware that pressing function key F12 from the Desktop should always invoke the command line (and as a result no application may use this key for its own purposes). If your task intercepts key presses but does not pass on unrecognised keys, then pressing F12 will have no effect at all as long as your task is in a position to respond to this reason code.

Because our program is merely a test program to indicate which key has been pressed, we are intercepting all key presses except F12, and the way the procedure is actually coded is not typical. Normally, however, you would only want to process a few particular keys, such as carriage returns, cursor keys and so on. The structure of your procedure would usually look something like this:

```
CASE key% OF
WHEN 13 :PROCdo_something
WHEN &181:PROCdo_something_else
WHEN ... :
OTHERWISE:SYS "Wimp_ProcessKey",key%
ENDCASE
```

MASKING EVENTS

We saw earlier that the circumstances under which reason code 6 is returned depend on the work area flags for the corresponding window, but there is another factor which determines exactly which reason codes are returned by the Wimp to each task. The **Wimp_Poll** call supplies a *mask* to the Wimp indicating which reason codes it wishes to receive in response to the call. If we set this mask to zero (as we have done so far in *OurTask*) then all codes will potentially be returned. It is good practice, however, to mask out the reason codes that your task does not want. This can speed up the responsiveness of the Wimp considerably - especially if you can mask out reason code zero, which will be returned very frequently in most cases.

Supplying the mask is easy; it is the R0 parameter passed to **Wimp_Poll**. To mask out reason codes 0, 4 and 5 in *OurTask*, we just need to alter line 510 as follows:

```
510 SYS "Wimp_Poll",1+(1<<4)+(1<<5),block% TO reason%
```

If you now run the program, you will see that the incrementing count no longer appears at the top of the screen, and there is no longer a sound generated when the pointer enters or leaves the window. As you may have guessed, the masking bit number corresponds exactly to the reason code number (bit 4 for reason code 4, etc.). The only proviso is that reason codes 2, 3, 7, 9, 10, and 13-16 cannot be masked, and their mask bits (together with bits 20-31) must be set to zero. Furthermore, three reason codes (1, 6 and 8) should not normally be masked, because the corresponding event will be queued until it is dealt with, and the Wimp will come to a halt in the meantime. The only reason for masking these events is to defer responding to them temporarily. Thus the only reason codes that may be masked out permanently are 0, 4, 5, 11, 12, 17, 18, 19.

Since the very essence of a Wimp program is its core of routines to respond to Wimp poll reason codes, we shall be meeting several of these codes again throughout the book, and indeed we will be describing in detail other reason codes which have not been covered in this chapter.

At this point in the book you should be beginning to get a feel for the Wimp and for the basic framework of a Wimp program. You should be able to see the fundamental difference between a multi-tasking program and any single-tasking program you have written before: the pivotal point of a Wimp program is its call to **Wimp_Poll**, and the rest of the program consists essentially of a set of procedures each of which is designed to handle the program's response to a reason code returned by this call.

If you feel that you are still floundering, we would suggest that you re-read this chapter very carefully, and if necessary re-read Chapter 2, and experiment some more with the listings provided.

Before we go on to icons and menus, Chapter 4 will digress slightly and discuss more fully a topic which we have already touched upon, and which needs to be fully understood at an early stage of Wimp programming: error handling.

4. Error Handling

Trapping errors - Reporting errors - Responding to error boxes - Example program

We have already introduced the subject of error handling very briefly in Chapter 1. It would have been impossible to do otherwise, since all Wimp programs should have some method for dealing with errors, as we explained earlier. We now need to look a little more closely at the subject.

TRAPPING ERRORS

As you will probably know if you have written Basic programs before, BBC Basic provides an *ON ERROR* statement which enables you to specify actions which should be taken if the program encounters an error of any kind. We have already seen this in use in *OurTask*:

```
 190 ON ERROR PROCerror(REPORT$+" at line "+STR$ERL):S
YS "Wimp_CloseDown":END
```

It is important to realise that Basic will not act on your error handler until the line which contains it has been executed, and also that any subsequent *ON ERROR* statement it meets will override the previous one. So it is quite possible to have a number of *ON ERROR* statements scattered throughout the program, each one giving directions to an error handler which caters for the specific needs of that section of the program.

Another feature of the statement which you must bear in mind is that, after encountering an error, Basic jumps to the statement following the *ON ERROR* which is currently in force, regardless of which section of the program is currently being executed. In other words, any error will cause Basic to forget all about what it was doing at the time (and this includes functions, procedures, loops etc.) and go straight back to the point at which the error handler was set up. You have to be very careful about this, since if this results in the same section of code which caused the error being executed again as a result of jumping back to the error handler, the program will enter an infinite loop from which the only escape is to reset the computer. To see this in practice, alter lines 190-200 of *!RunImage* as follows:

```
190 ON ERROR PROCerror(REPORT$+" at line "+STR$ERL)
200 whandle%=FNcreatewindow(200,200,300,500,200,200)
```

What we have done here is to remove the instruction to terminate the task from the error handler, and introduce an error into line 200 by omitting the underscore character between "create" and "window". What will now happen is that as soon as Basic reaches line 200, it will detect the error and pass control back to the statement following *ON ERROR*, in this case the call to *PROCerror*. The next statement after this is, of course, the one which caused the error, so the whole cycle will be repeated endlessly. You can only get out of this by resetting the computer, for example by pressing Ctrl-Break, so don't try this experiment if you have any unsaved data in any other applications at the time.

Error handling in Basic is quite a complex subject, and it is recommended that you read the relevant sections of the *BBC Basic Guide* for full details. However, in its simplest form, by using one or more *ON ERROR* statements as we have done here, it will meet the needs of a good many Wimp programs.

In *OurTask*, we have placed the error handler immediately after the call to **Wimp_Initialise**, so it will handle any errors generated while the program is running under the control of the Wimp. It is not uncommon to include an earlier error handler which is specifically designed to pick up errors *before* that point. For example, you could include the following line in the program to do this:

```
65 ON ERROR PRINT REPORT$;" at line ";ERL:END
```

REPORTING ERRORS

Before we describe the SWI call **Wimp_ReportError**, it is important to realise that the call itself knows nothing about the error it is asked to report. In other words, it is not an error handler itself but is provided for the use of error handlers. This means that it is not restricted to reporting errors which Basic has encountered, but may be used by your program to report any errors of its own, completely independently of any error handlers you may have set up. For example, if your program requires the user to type a value into a writable icon, and you want to restrict that value (which we will assume is now held in a variable *val%*) to a maximum of 20, you could include the following line in your code immediately after ascertaining the value of *val%*:

```
IF val%>20 THEN PROCerror("The number is too large")
```

We will be showing you how to read an icon's contents when we look at icons in the next chapter.

As an incidental but interesting aside, this little example illustrates perfectly the difference between a Wimp and a non-Wimp program. You will probably have written programs in the past which require user input, and you may well be used to writing loops which repeat until the correct value has been entered, as for example:

```
REPEAT INPUT val%
IF val%>20 PRINT "Number too large"
UNTIL val%<=20
```

You must *never, ever* do this under the Wimp. All user input is handled by calling **Wimp_Poll**, and it is very bad programming practice to have a second poll loop within the main one. You must, therefore, treat each response from **Wimp_Poll** as your input loop, and not set up your own inside it.

On entry:
R0 = pointer to error block
R1 = flags
R2 = pointer to application name
(for error box title)

On exit:
R1 = user response

Figure 4.1
Details of SWI
"Wimp_ReportError" (&400DF)

The parameters required by **Wimp_ReportError** are shown in figure 4.1. We have already touched on these towards the end of Chapter 1, and you will remember that R0 must point to an error block. The first four bytes of this block contain the error number, and in our program we have used a number of 255. This is purely and simply because this number is not used elsewhere. In theory, error numbers can cover the entire 4-byte range available, i.e. 0 to &FFFFFFFF. In practice, only a small proportion of these are actually used. Acorn has split the numbers into chunks, each of which is allocated to a particular part of the operating system or to a software producer. Unless you are writing commercial applications, it is not necessary to worry too much about error numbers, and we will continue to use 255 in our program.

The error number is followed immediately in the block by a string containing the message which is to be displayed in the error box. You will notice that this string must be null terminated, i.e. it must end with a zero byte (ASCII 0). This serves to highlight an important factor which you must bear in mind when programming the Wimp. If you have written programs in Basic you will be aware that strings are normally terminated by a carriage return (ASCII 13). However, many SWI calls under RISC OS which operate on strings expect those strings to be terminated by a zero byte, and will also terminate with zero any strings returned by the call. Writing a Wimp program in Basic, therefore, requires that any such strings have a zero byte added to the end before being passed to the SWI call, and similarly any strings returned must be passed through a function which replaces the zero with a carriage return. If this is not done, Basic will simply not recognise the set of bytes as a string. We will meet a function to do this later in the book.

The flags word passed to **Wimp_ReportError** in R1 requires a little bit of explanation. Seven of the bits in this word may be set or unset in order to convey certain information about the way in which the error box is displayed or subsequently handled. Only three of these bits are likely to be of any real use for most programs, and these are shown in Figure 4.2.

Bit	Meaning when set
0	Provide an OK icon
1	Provide a Cancel icon
4	Don't prefix the application name with "Error from"

Figure 4.2
Some useful flags for Wimp_ReportError

So far in our program we have used a flag value of 1 (bit 0 set) which has resulted in an OK icon appearing, and a title bar for the error box which reads "Error from OurTask" (since "OurTask" was the string we passed in R2). But we could have used a flag value of 3, which would have displayed both an OK and a Cancel icon, or a value of 19, which would have displayed OK and Cancel icons, and a title which read simply "OurTask". This could have been expanded by passing as the string in R2 "Warning from OurTask" or any other title message we chose. Note that the Wimp will automatically display an OK icon anyway if neither bit 0 nor bit 1 is set.

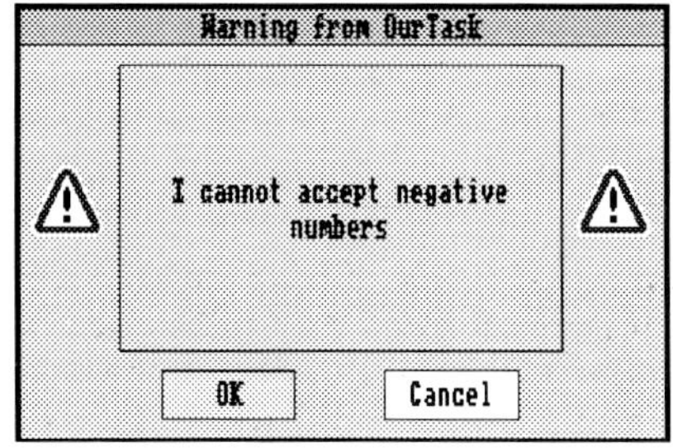

An error box with user-defined title

RESPONDING TO ERROR BOXES

You will have noticed that when an error box is displayed, the whole operation of the computer is suspended until the user clicks on one of the icons (OK or Cancel if present). This is fine as long as there is only one icon - it is obvious when the user has clicked because control returns to the program. But what if both OK and Cancel icons are present - how do we know which has been selected? The answer is that a value is returned in R1. This will be 1 if OK is selected, or 2 if it is Cancel. In this way, you can build in a choice of actions if necessary. To give you an example, alter the *OurTask* program as follows and then run it:

```
85 ON ERROR PROCerror(REPORT$)
95 x%=val%
750 SYS "Wimp_ReportError",block%,3,app$ TO ,errclic
k%
755 IF errclick%=1 THEN val%=0
```

What will happen now is that the error handler in line 85 will take over from the earlier one in line 190. When line 95 is reached the first time round the poll loop, an "Unknown or missing variable" error will be reported, because the variable *val%* has not yet been declared. The error box will now show both OK and Cancel icons, because we have altered the value of the flags in line 750, and we have also added a return value for R1 which is decoded by line 755. If you click on OK, then *val%* is defined, which means that next time round the poll loop there will no longer be an error and the program will continue as normal. However, if you click on Cancel before you have clicked on OK, the error will be reported again since the variable has not been defined.

The difference between the actions taken when clicking on either of these icons will depend on the task itself. Normally the task will assume that if Cancel is clicked, the user wishes to abort the current operation, while if OK is clicked, the user wishes to go ahead despite the error. For a good many error reporting situations a choice is unnecessary, and a single OK icon is adequate in order to resume operation of the program, or in the case of a serious error, to terminate it.

EXAMPLE PROGRAM

We will now update the *OurTask* program to take account of the features of **Wimp_ReportError** which have been covered here. As usual, this listing should be added to the earlier ones. We have included lines 85, 95 and 755 as blank lines in case you have experimented with them as described above.

Listing 4.1

```
   30 REM Updated to Chapter 4
   85
   95
  190 ON ERROR PROCerror(REPORT$+" at line "+STR$ERL)
  700 DEF PROCreport(err$,flag%)
  710 name$=app$
  720 IF flag% AND 16 THEN name$="Message from "+name$
  750 SYS "Wimp_ReportError",block%,flag%,name$ TO ,er
rclick%
  755
  800 DEF PROCerror(a$)
  810 PROCreport(a$,1)
  820 SYS "Wimp_CloseDown"
  830 END
  840 ENDPROC
  850 :
 1560 PROCreport("You have clicked the "+a$+" button",
19)
 1570 IF errclick%=2 SYS "Wimp_CloseDown":END
 1730 PROCreport("You have pressed a key - ASCII code
"+STR$key%+" (hex &"+STR$~key%+")",19)
 1735 IF errclick%=2 SYS "Wimp_CloseDown":END
```

The effect of adding this listing is to make two major changes to the way in which the program works. Firstly, you will see that we have now renamed the original *PROCerror* as *PROCreport*, and added a new *PROCerror*. This now enables us to differentiate between errors reported by Basic (which are passed to the new *PROCerror*) and errors or messages which we generate ourselves. *PROCreport* carries out the function of calling **Wimp_ReportError** and then passes control back to the point from which it was called, allowing the program to decode the response and act upon it. On the other hand, *PROCerror* itself calls *PROCreport* but then terminates the task as soon as the user responds.

The other change is that an additional parameter has been added to *PROCreport*, which is the flags byte. This allows you to decide at the point of calling the procedure whether to include a Cancel icon, or whether to avoid the words "Error from".

Line 180, the general error handler, no longer needs to terminate the task since this is now done by *PROCerror* itself. Two additional lines have been added to *PROCreport* - 710 and 720. These determine whether bit 4 of the flags byte is set, and if it is, the application name is prefaced by "Message from ". The two lines which previously reported an error when a button was clicked or a key pressed (1560 and 1730), now set bit 4 of the flags so that these actions are no longer described as errors. Furthermore, both OK and Cancel icons are now provided; clicking on OK continues with the normal operation of the task, while clicking on Cancel terminates it.

There is little more we need to say at present about error handling, but you will see plenty more examples as the program builds up over the chapters. In Chapter 5 we will get back to the Wimp itself and tackle the subject of icons.

5. Icons

Icons in use - Creating icons - Example program - Icon flags - Indirected icons - Exclusive selection groups - Menu icons - Radio icons - Writable icons - Altering icons - Validation - Sprite icons - The icon bar

We are now ready to move on to the next element in our "WIMP" acronym. Icons form a vital part of any Wimp system, and in Acorn's window manager the icon is a powerful and flexible component. Because of this flexibility, this chapter contains a substantial amount of information, and we recommend that you try to absorb it in stages in order to grasp fully all the concepts which are introduced.

An icon is defined in the PRM simply as "a rectangular area of a window's workspace", and can contain a sprite or text, or a combination of both. The sprites appearing in directory displays on the Desktop are all icons, but icons can take many other forms. Each item in a Wimp menu is also an icon. In this case the icons are usually text only, though it is also possible to use sprites. Any icon can behave in a wide variety of different ways. For example, it might have its foreground and background colours reversed when the pointer moves over it or when it is selected by clicking; it might be greyed out to show that it cannot be selected; it might be set up to notify the task if the user double-clicks over it; or it might be what is termed a *writable icon,* which means that you can type text into it, and edit the result. All these functions are controlled automatically by the Wimp; all you have to do is set the appropriate flags when creating the icon, as we shall see in this chapter.

ICONS IN USE

The *Paint* application offers a good example of icons being used in a practical situation. Load or create a sprite in Paint, open the sprite window ready for editing, and choose the *Show tools* option from the *Paint* submenu. You should now see the *Paint Tools* window, which is shown in Figure 5.1, and is full of icons. In the top section of the window are 21 sprite icons representing graphically the various functions that can be selected from the window. Below these is a text icon, whose text changes to show which function is currently selected, and below this are a further four text icons, labelled "Set", "OR", "AND" and "EOR". The text in these does not change, but you will notice that if you click on one of these icons, its colours are reversed, while the colours of the other three stay as (or revert to) the normal colouring.

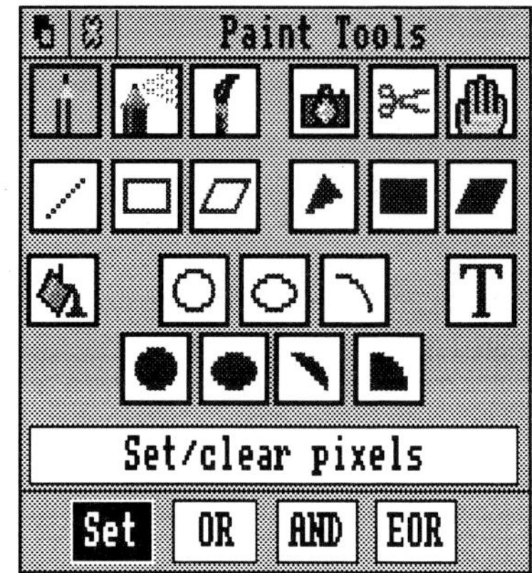

Figure 5.1
Paint's Paint Tools *window*

Now select the *Insert text* function (by clicking on the T icon). An extension to the window appears containing eight more icons. Four of these are plain text icons with no borders and with their background colour set to the same as the window's work area. The remainder are writable icons, and you will find that clicking on one of these displays the caret (the red vertical bar) in that icon, whereupon you can type and edit text as long as the caret is visible.

CREATING ICONS

Icons are always associated with a parent window, and each window can have many icons within it, as we have just seen. Each icon has an icon handle unique within its own window (issued by the Wimp in incrementing values from zero), so that the window and icon handles together uniquely define the icon.

We mentioned briefly in Chapter 2 that icons can be created as part of the window creation process, by adding the icon definitions to the end of the parameter block for **Wimp_CreateWindow**. They can also be created separately by using the call **Wimp_CreateIcon** (SWI &400C2). This is analogous to **Wimp_CreateWindow**, in that it informs the Wimp about the icon and supplies all the flags necessary to define it completely without actually displaying it on the screen. This only occurs when the parent window or the icon itself is updated.

The information required by the Wimp to create an icon is exactly the same whether you use **Wimp_CreateIcon** or include it in **Wimp_CreateWindow**. In the former case, a 36-byte parameter block is set up (with the address passed in R1 as usual). This is shown in Figure 5.2, and consists of 4 bytes giving the window handle followed by a 32-byte icon definition block. In the case of **Wimp_CreateWindow** this 32-byte block is appended to the end of the window parameter block (and repeated for as many icons as you wish to create at that time). Obviously the Wimp needs to know in this case how many icon definitions are appended, and to do this you simply alter the value at block+84 (see Figure 2.3 in Chapter 2). We will explain the meaning of the elements within the icon definition block shortly. Note that if you are creating icons with **Wimp_CreateWindow**, the Wimp does not return icon handles - it merely allocates handle 0 to the first icon in the list, handle 1 to the next and so on. It is the responsibility of the task to know which is which.

Parameter block pointed to by R1:

block+0	Handle of window (or -2 for left of icon bar, -1 for right)
4	Minimum x co-ordinate of icon bounding box
8	Minimum y co-ordinate of icon bounding box
12	Maximum x co-ordinate of icon bounding box
16	Maximum y co-ordinate of icon bounding box
20	Icon flags
24	12 bytes of icon data

The call returns the icon handle in R0

Figure 5.2
Details of SWI "Wimp_CreateIcon" (&400C2)

EXAMPLE PROGRAM

Typically the parent window would be created, either together with or followed by all its icons, then the window would be opened by using a call to **Wimp_OpenWindow** as described in Chapter 2. Some properties of icons can be altered, and indeed new icons can be created, at later stages in the process as we shall see in due course. But before we go any further we will update *OurTask* to create its first icon. Add Listing 5.1 to the existing *!RunImage* program in the usual way, and then run the application. You should now see an icon towards the top left corner of the window. Notice that if you drag the window around, the icon moves with it - all this is done automatically by the Wimp and needs no help from the task whatsoever. Notice, too, that we have now masked out poll reason codes 0, 4 and 5 (by altering the mask in line 510), removed the code which displayed the incrementing count on the screen, and also unset the hot keys bit in the window flags in line 1140.

Listing 5.1

```
  165
  240 i0handle%=FNcreate_icon(whandle%,32,-100,160,48,
&700303D,"Test icon",0,0,0)
  510 SYS "Wimp_Poll",&31,block% TO reason%
  530
  600 WHEN 6:PROCclick(block%!16)
 1140 block%!28=&FF000012
 1500 DEF PROCclick(icon%)
 1510 CASE icon% OF
 1520 WHEN -1:a$="the background"
 1530 OTHERWISE:a$="icon "+STR$icon%
 1540
 1560 PROCreport("You have clicked over "+a$,19)
 2000 DEF FNcreate_icon(whan%,ix%,iy%,iw%,ih%,flag%,te
xt$,ptr1%,ptr2%,ptr3%)
 2010 !block%=whan%
 2020 block%!4=ix%
 2030 block%!8=iy%
 2040 block%!12=ix%+iw%
 2050 block%!16=iy%+ih%
 2060 block%!20=flag%
 2080 $(block%+24)=text$
 2140 SYS "Wimp_CreateIcon",,block% TO ihandle%
 2150 =ihandle%
 2160 :
```

If you have followed the build-up of our program over the course of the book so far, you should not have too much difficulty in understanding the function *FNcreate_icon*. This is called at line 240 and takes ten parameters, of which the first five are the window handle, the x and y co-ordinates of the bottom left-hand corner of the icon, and the icon's width and height respectively. These are all placed into the block in lines 2010-2050. The four co-ordinates are all measured relative to the window's work area origin, i.e. the top left-hand corner of the work area, so the y co-ordinates of the icon bounding box are measured downwards and will both be negative, with the more negative of the two being first - see figure 5.3. As with our window creation function, we have specified the second pair of parameters as width and height rather than the co-ordinates of the top right-hand corner of the icon, and so we must add them to the x and y co-ordinates of the bottom left corner in order to supply the correct values for **Wimp_CreateIcon**.

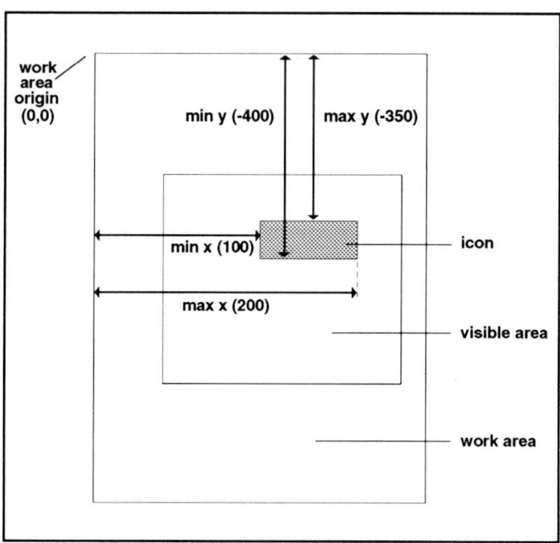

Figure 5.3
The four co-ordinates used in the Wimp_CreateIcon parameter block, with example values

ICON FLAGS

The remaining five parameters to *FNcreate_icon* require some explanation, and we will start with the icon flags, passed to the function in *flag%*. The 32 bits of icon flag data are shown in Figure 5.4. Most of the items should by now be reasonably obvious, but there are three which call for comment. If bit 8 is set, the icon data is *indirected*. This means that instead of the icon text (or the name of the sprite) itself being placed at block+24, the block holds a pointer to an area of RAM. This permits text of more than 12 characters in length to be used in an icon, and also allows the creation of icons containing both text and a sprite. Additionally, indirection *must* be used in cases where the content of the icon is liable to change (such as with writable icons), and in other special cases. We will be looking at indirected icons later in the chapter.

Bit	Meaning when set
0	Icon contains text
1	Icon contains a sprite
2	Icon has a border
3	Contents centred horizontally
4	Contents centred vertically
5	Icon has filled background
6	Text is anti-aliased
7	Icon requires task's help for redraw
8	Icon data is indirected
9	Text is right justified
10	If selected with Adjust don't cancel others in same ESG
11	Display sprite at half size
12-15	Icon button type
16-20	Exclusive selection group (ESG)
21	Icon is (already) selected
22	Icon is not selectable (is shaded)
23	Icon has been deleted
24-27	Foreground colour (if bit 6=0)
28-31	Background colour (if bit 6=0)
24-31	Font handle (if bit 6=1)

Figure 5.4
Icon flags used with Wimp_CreateIcon

The second point that needs clarification is the notion of an *exclusive selection group* or ESG (bits 10 and 16-20). The Wimp allows you to nominate groups of icons whose behaviour can depend on the state of others in the same group. For example, you might have a feature which could take three possible values (thus volume might be high, low or off). In such a case icons representing the three states could be placed in the same ESG by giving them the same ESG number (i.e. any number between 1 and 31, since the value supplied at bits 16-20 is a five-bit integer). Each time one of the icons in that group is selected, the Wimp will automatically deselect all other icons in the same group. Any icon with an ESG of zero on the other hand will behave independently of all others. Again we will take a closer look at this feature later in the chapter.

Finally the icon button type is again an integer value, this time a number between 0 and 15 which specifies how the icon will affect, and be affected by, the pointer. Figure 5.5 shows the range of icon button types and the action associated with each.

Value	Effect
0	Ignore the mouse and pointer
1	Notify task continuously while pointer is over icon
2	Click notifies task (auto repeat)
3	Click notifies task (once only)
4	Click selects icon; release over icon notifies task; moving pointer away deselects
5	Click selects; double-click notifies task
6	As 3 but can also drag
7	As 4 but can also drag (moving away doesn't deselect)
8	As 5 but can also drag
9	Pointer over icon selects; moving away deselects; click over icon notifies task (*menu icon*)
10	Click returns button state*256; drag returns button state*16; double-click returns button state*1
11	Click selects, and returns button state*1; drag returns button state*16 (*radio icon*)
12-13	Reserved
14	Click causes icon to gain caret, and parent window to gain input focus (*writable icon*); can also drag
15	Click causes icon to gain caret, and parent window to gain input focus (*writable icon*)

Figure 5.5
Icon button types

You should notice a strong similarity between the icon button type and the work area flags which we looked at in Chapter 2 (see Figure 2.9), and in fact the two work in a very similar way. *Menu icons*, *radio icons* and *writable icons* all have particular properties which are recognised by the Wimp, and we will elaborate on these later.

ICON FLAG GENERATOR

It is a good idea at this point to experiment with the values passed to *FNcreate_icon* for the icon flags and the bounding box co-ordinates. Because of the complexity of deriving valid icon flags, the program in Listing 5.7 at the end of the chapter is supplied. This attempts to automate the process. If you run it, it first asks if you have a default set of flags (which you may wish to use as a template for a new set). If you just press Return at this point, the default option will be ignored. But if you supply a set of icon flags as a hex number, this will be used as a default in what follows.

You will then be presented with each icon attribute, and will be asked to enter Y, N or a numerical value where appropriate. By pressing Return on any item, you will enter the default from the default string supplied at the start. At the end a hex value is displayed for the resultant set of flags, which should then be inserted into line 230 in place of the original value of &700303D. You may like to try altering the colours of the icon, the alignment of the text, whether it has a border or is filled, and the text itself (though it must not at this stage be more than 12 characters long).

You could also experiment with the icon button type. Try a value of 0 (&700003D in the icon flags byte) and see what happens when you click on the icon. Then try a value of 15 (&700F03D) and repeat the test. You could also try a value of 9 (&700903D) and see what happens then. If the ESG is still set to 0 you will probably find that the last-mentioned button type produces an odd effect - try altering the ESG to a non-zero value with a button type of 9 (e.g. &701903D) and you should see a behaviour pattern which you will recognise from menu structures, and from icons used in some applications.

INDIRECTED ICONS

We have purposely kept our program simple so far and have not yet catered for indirected icons. In Listing 5.1, we simply put the text string directly into the block in line 2080, using our seventh function parameter, *text$*:

```
2080 $(block%+24)=text$
```

In many cases, this is all we need to do, since 12 characters is often enough to hold the text that we wish to display, and will always be enough to hold the name of a sprite. However, it is often necessary for an icon to hold more than 12 characters of text, and furthermore, data held directly in the parameter block in this way cannot be altered once the icon has been created. So an alternative method is provided for specifying text or sprite names which cannot be handled in the normal way. This is known as *indirection*. Indirection means simply that instead of the data itself appearing in the block, a pointer to a data block elsewhere in RAM is supplied. The contents of this data block are set up by the task, and can be altered at any point in the program.

In fact, since there are 12 bytes available at block+24, three pointers are supplied, and these form the last three parameters to *FNcreate_icon*, which are *ptr1%*, *ptr2%* and *ptr3%*. The exact use to which the three data words is put depends on the state of three bits in the icon flags: bit 8 (indirection), bit 1 (sprite) and bit 0 (text). Bit 8 *must* be set, otherwise indirection is not used. The effect of the other two bits on an indirected icon is given in Figure 5.6.

Sprite	Text	Use of the 3 data words	
0	1	+24	Pointer to text buffer
		+28	Pointer to validation string
		+32	Text buffer length
1	0	+24	Pointer to sprite or sprite name
		+28	Pointer to sprite control block (+1 for Wimp sprite area)
		+32	0 if +24 is a sprite pointer, length if it's a name pointer
1	1	+24	Pointer to text buffer
		+28	Pointer to validation string, which can contain sprite name
		+32	Text buffer length

Figure 5.6
The meaning of the 3 data words depends on the state of the sprite and text bits in the icon flags.
The address of the 3 words is given as an offset from the address in R1 (the start of the parameter block)

To take the two cases where the text bit is set (for text or text-plus-sprite icons), the first of these words (block+24) is a pointer to a text string elsewhere in memory, while the third (block+32) is the length of the buffer used for this string (i.e. the maximum number of characters that can be displayed in the icon). The pointer in the middle (block+28) is to a so-called *validation string* which enables you to specify information about the format of the text string - we will look at this later but for the moment we will not complicate matters by describing it here, except to say that in the case of a text-plus-sprite icon the validation string will contain the sprite name if applicable.

In the case of sprite icons, the first pointer is to a buffer containing the sprite name, or a pointer to a sprite itself. The second points to a sprite control block (which may be an explicit reference to a block set up by the task itself, or it may point to the Wimp sprite pool if a value of 1 is used instead of a pointer). The third pointer is either zero (if the first pointer points to a sprite) or the buffer length if it points to a buffer containing the name.

To help clarify this we will add a simple example to our program. Suppose we wish to create an icon containing the text string "Serial port status". Because this is more than 12 characters in length, we must use an indirected icon. We must first derive a value for the icon flags for our new icon. If we take as a basis the flags word used in our earlier example, (&700303D), the only change we need to make is to set the indirection flag (at bit 8). We can do this by adding 2^8 (=&100) to the original value. This gives a new flag value of &700313D.

This new icon is still text only, so the sprite bit is zero. This means that the three data words take the form given in the first of the three entries in figure 5.6 (i.e. sprite=0, text=1). This tells us that the first word must point to the text string in memory, the second to a validation string (we will set this to -1 because no validation string is used in this example), while the third simply gives the text buffer length.

Listing 5.2

```
  210 DIM text1% 32
  220 $text1%="Serial port status"
  250 i1handle%=FNcreate_icon(whandle%,32,-200,300,48,
&700313D,"",text1%,-1,32)
 2070 IF ptr1%=0 THEN
 2090 ELSE
 2100 block%!24=ptr1%
 2110 block%!28=ptr2%
 2120 block%!32=ptr3%
 2130 ENDIF
```

What we have done here is to dimension a small text buffer, *text1%* (line 210) and place our text string into it (line 220). Our new call to *FNcreate_icon* in line 250 places the icon at co-ordinates 32,-200 within the work area, and gives it a width of 300 graphics units and a height of 48. Now if you run the program you will see the new icon, but you will notice that part of it lies beyond the edge of the visible area. To rectify this, alter the line which determines the size of the visible area as follows:

```
200 whandle%=FNcreate_window(200,200,400,500,100,200)
```

EXCLUSIVE SELECTION GROUPS

When an icon is initially defined, it is assigned to a so-called *exclusive selection group* (or ESG) by supplying a number between 0 and 31 in the icon flags (bits 16-20). If zero is used, then the ESG feature does not take effect, but for any other value, the Wimp ensures that only one member of each group may be highlighted at any time. Thus if you assign three icons to ESG 1, selecting any one of them by clicking on it with Select will cause the other two icons in the same group to be deselected automatically.

The effect of clicking with Adjust depends on the state of icon flag 10. If this is set, then selecting an icon with a non-zero ESG does not de-select the others in the group. You can see this in operation when selecting files in a directory display.

We can easily set up an ESG in the test program. As it stands at the moment, both icons have been assigned to ESG 0, making them behave independently. But we can assign them to ESG 1 by altering the value of the integer in bits 16-20 of their icon flags from a zero to a one. At the same time, we will alter the button type to 5 (click selects; double-click notifies task). Thus &700303D becomes &701503D, and &700313D becomes &701513D. So now insert these values into lines 240 and 250 as follows:

```
  240 i0handle%=FNcreate_icon(whandle%,32,-100,160,48,
&701503D,"Test icon",0,0,0)
  250 i1handle%=FNcreate_icon(whandle%,32,-200,300,48,
&701513D,"",text1%,-1,32)
```

If you now run the program, you will see that if one is highlighted, clicking on the other will de-highlight it, and so on. Furthermore, a single click will no longer activate the error box as before, whereas a double-click on either icon will do so. At the moment clicking with Adjust will have exactly the same effect as clicking with Select. But if you now set flag 10, by altering the value of the flags to &701543D in line 240 and &701553D in line 250, you will find that the two icons are no longer mutually exclusive when clicking with Adjust.

As it stands, when the test application starts up neither of the two icons is in a selected state. To remedy this, we can set flag 21 of one of the icons at the start of the program. In the case of the first icon (line 240), this involves changing its flag to &721543D.

MENU ICONS

We mentioned earlier that there are three particular types of icon which the Wimp recognises as having special properties. The first of these types is known as the *menu icon* (button type 9). When the pointer moves over an icon of this type, it is "selected" (i.e. the colours are inverted), and when the pointer moves away it is deselected. If the mouse is clicked while the icon is selected, then the task is notified. It is called a menu icon because this is exactly what happens when you traverse a RISC OS menu; in fact, menu items are nothing more than icons whose button type is forced by the Wimp to type 9.

If you experimented earlier with button types as we suggested, you may have tried out type 9 and found that the colours flickered continually while the pointer was over the icon. This is because, in order to use this button type effectively, you must set the ESG to a non-zero value. This can be any value between 1 and 31, and all menu icons in a window can have the same ESG since by their very nature only one can be selected at any time. It is usual therefore to keep one ESG number specifically for all menu icons in a window, using other non-zero ESG numbers for cases where icons need to be grouped (see the section below on radio icons), while all remaining icons in the window will be set to an ESG of zero.

Menu icons are often used where a click is required to confirm or cancel an action within a dialogue box. To take a concrete example, load up Paint once more, open a sprite file window, and move the pointer across the *Create* option on the menu in order to display the *Create Sprite* dialogue box. If you now move the pointer over the *OK* icon, you will see that it is a menu icon, and behaves exactly as we have described here.

RADIO ICONS

Radio icons (button type 11) allow you to group a set of icons in such a way that when one is selected, all the others in the same group are deselected. As such, they make use of the properties of ESGs which we have described earlier, and which we have already seen in our test program. Unlike button type 5 which we used in the test program, however, clicking with Select on a radio icon which is already selected does not de-select it. The icons therefore behave like a row of buttons on a radio set for selecting the waveband - hence the name "radio icon". Clearly, all icons in a group must have the same ESG number, and this number must be unique to the group within the window.

It is quite common to use text-plus-sprite icons for radio icons. Acorn has in fact provided a pair of sprites for this very purpose; these have the appearance of a white diamond shape, which turns green in the centre when selected (see Figure 5.7). You can see two groups of these icons in Paint's *Print Sprite* window (to see this, load or create a sprite and then move the pointer across the *Print* menu option). We will be showing you how to use sprites in icons later in this chapter.

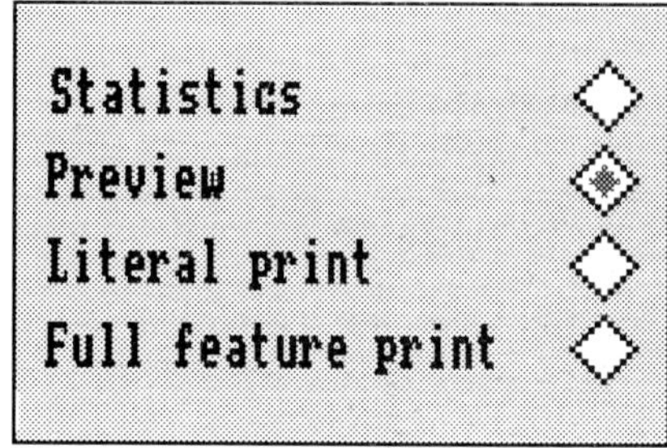

Figure 5.7
A group of radio icons using Acorn's sprites

If we now change the icon definitions in our program, we can see the effect of various types of icon within the same window. Add Listing 5.3 to our *!RunImage* program and then run it.

Listing 5.3

```
  210
  220
  240 i0handle%=FNcreate_icon(whandle%,32,-100,128,48,
&7000019,"Volume:",0,0,0)
  250 i1handle%=FNcreate_icon(whandle%,180,-100,80,48,
&722B03D,"High",0,0,0)
  260 i2handle%=FNcreate_icon(whandle%,180,-160,80,48,
&702B03D,"Low",0,0,0)
  270 i3handle%=FNcreate_icon(whandle%,80,-300,120,64,
&C701903D,"OK",0,0,0)
 1505 IF block%!8 AND 5 THEN
 1520 WHEN 1:PROCreport("High is now set",17)
 1530 WHEN 2:PROCreport("Low is now set",17)
 1540 WHEN 3:PROCreport("You have clicked on OK",17)
 1560
 1570 ENDIF
```

Icon 0 is now a plain text icon (type 0) bearing the legend "Volume:", while icons 1 and 2 ("High" and "Low") are radio icons in ESG 2, and icon 3 is a menu icon in ESG 1 containing the text "OK". When you run the program, you will now find that it is starting to behave like a real application. Clicking on *Volume* or on the background has no effect, because normally these would not require any action by a program. Clicking on *High* or *Low* will display a message telling you which has been selected, while clicking on OK also displays a message reporting the click. This all takes place because we have altered the actions of *PROCclick*. In a real application, the calls to *PROCreport* in lines 1520-1540 would be replaced by code which performed some action dependent on which icon had been clicked.

WRITABLE ICONS

A *writable icon* (button type 15) is exactly what the word suggests: an icon into which text may be typed by the user. You will see writable icons in use on the Desktop whenever you perform a save operation for example, as the icon into which you must enter the filename is of this type. This form of icon makes life very easy for the programmer, because all the text input and editing performed by the user is handled entirely by the Wimp, and the task only becomes involved if Return or certain special keys are pressed (see Figure 3.5 in Chapter 3 for a list of these). In other words, if any key other than those just mentioned is pressed while the caret is in a writable icon, the Wimp will enter the appropriate character into the icon without bothering to inform the task of the keypress. This includes processing keys such as Delete, Copy, Cursor left and Cursor right, and Ctrl-U (which deletes the entire text in the icon).

To see how this works, we will create a simple writable icon in our program. We will need to dimension another small buffer, but this time we will put an empty string into the buffer to start with:

```
210 DIM text1% 20:$text1%=""
```

though it could contain anything you wish up to a maximum length of the buffer size (in this case 21) less 1 for the terminator. For example, writable icons in save boxes are often set up initially with a default filename, such as *SpriteFile* or *TextFile*.

Next we need to define another icon with a suitable set of icon flags. We can base these on the value used previously for our indirected icon (&700313D). A writable icon has to be indirected since otherwise it would not be possible for the change in contents to be registered as the user types in text. The only alteration we need to make to the flags is in the icon button type. This was previously type 3, but we now need type 15. If you use the Icon Flag

Generator and enter the previous value as a starting point, you will get a new value of &700F13D, so you can now add the following lines to the test program:

```
210 DIM text1% 20:$text1%=""
280 i4handle%=FNcreate_icon(whandle%,8,-400,384,48,&7
00F13D,"",text1%,-1,21)
```

When you run the program, you will see the new icon, which will be empty to start with. But as soon as you click the mouse over the icon, the red caret (a vertical cursor) appears, and the window surround turns cream in colour to indicate that this window, and this window alone, has the so-called *input focus*. Any text you type in will be written into this icon, and you may edit the text using the keys mentioned above. If you press keys which are not processed automatically by the Wimp (such as the function keys, Return etc.), these key presses will be reported to the task by the Wimp using reason code 8, and so the procedure we inserted into *OurTask* back in Chapter 3 to handle these reason codes (*PROCkeypress*) will now be activated again.

This demonstrates that, for normal text entry in a writable icon, everything is handled by the Wimp without further ado, but as soon as a key is pressed which needs attention, the task is asked to handle it. Pressing Return, for example, would mean that the user has finished typing into that particular icon, so the task may want to process the result. Pressing Cursor up or Cursor down may mean that the user wishes to move on to the next or previous writable icon in a chain, and so on. In a fully-fledged application, the task will need to respond to key presses such as these.

You will find if you have entered the lines exactly as given above that you cannot type more than 20 characters into the icon, even though there would be enough space for more. This is because we have specified the length of the buffer (the final parameter to *FNcreate_icon* and the pointer at block+32) as 21 (i.e. 20 characters plus a terminator).

You may notice that when it first appears, the caret is centred horizontally within the icon, and as you type in text or delete it, it remains centred. This is because we have set bit 3 of the icon flags for this icon (Horizontally centred). To justify the text to the right-hand end of the icon, we need to unset bit 3 and set bit 9 (Right justify). Probably the most common state is to use left justified text in writable icons. This is achieved by clearing both bits 3 and 9. To do this with the present icon, we would need to change the icon flags value to &700F135.

READING AND ALTERING THE CURRENT STATE OF AN ICON

Of course, there is not much point in letting the user type in text if the task doesn't know what has been written. In the example given here, this is easy: it is stored in the indirected text buffer set up at the start of the program. The string held at *text1%* will always reflect what the user has typed (because the Wimp has been given this address as the pointer to the icon's contents), and may be read at any time.

There are situations however (which we shall cover later in the book) where you may not know the address of the buffer being used for the icon's contents. You may also want to find out other information about the current state of an icon, or indeed alter its state in some way. To enable you to do this, the Wimp provides two SWI calls, **Wimp_GetIconState** (&400CE) and **Wimp_SetIconState** (&400CD). The first of these two calls returns the complete icon definition block updated to show the current state of the icon. To call **Wimp_GetIconState**, the window handle is placed at block+0 and the icon handle at block+4. The block address is passed in R1 as usual. On return these 8 bytes are preserved, and the 32-byte icon block is placed at block+8. Thus the minimum x co-ordinate of the icon's bounding box appears at block+8, the y co-ordinate at block+12, and so on. The icon flags (returned at block+24) can be used to check whether the icon is in a selected or deselected state (bit 21), whether it is shaded (bit 22) and so on.

If you do not know it already, you can also find out the address of an indirected icon's buffer by reading the contents of block+28. Remember that this is a *pointer* to the buffer, not the buffer itself, so you must read the string at block!28, not block+28. The following example shows how this would be done:

```
!block%=whandle%:block%!4=ihandle%
SYS "Wimp_GetIconState",,block%
icontext$=$(block%!28)
```

We mentioned earlier that you can alter parts of an icon's definition after it has been created. In fact, apart from the data in an indirected icon's buffer (which is not actually part of the icon definition itself), the only element that can be changed is the value of the icon flags. The SWI **Wimp_SetIconState** is provided to enable you to do this, and when this call is made the Wimp automatically updates the icon to reflect any changes that have been made. Details of the call are shown in Figure 5.8. The two values at block+8 and block+12 require some further explanation, and this is given in Figure 5.9. These two words taken together tell the Wimp exactly what to do with each bit of the icon flags. Any flags which are to be left alone must remain as zero in both words; any which are to be set must be 1 in both words; while any which are to be cleared must be 1 at block+12 and zero at block+8. A couple of examples will clarify this. Suppose we wish to set bit 22 (icon is to be shaded). This means that bit 22 must be 1 in both words, but all other bits must be zero. So the following lines will achieve this:

```
!block%=whandle%:block%!4=ihandle%
block%!8=1<<22:block%!12=1<<22
SYS "Wimp_SetIconState",,block%
```

If on the other hand we wished to unset bit 9 (text is right-justified) we would use:

```
!block%=whandle%:block%!4=ihandle%
block%!8=0:block%!12=1<<9
SYS "Wimp_SetIconState",,block%
```

block+0	window handle (-1 for icon bar right, -2 for icon bar left)
4	icon handle
8	EOR word
12	clear word

Figure 5.8
Parameter block for SWI "Wimp_SetIconState" (&400CD)

C	E	Effect
0	0	preserve the bit's status
0	1	toggle the bit's status
1	0	clear the bit
1	1	set the bit

Figure 5.9
Details of (C)lear word and (E)OR word for Wimp_SetIconState

VALIDATION

We mentioned earlier that an indirected icon can employ a *validation string*. This string can serve a number of functions. For example, you can use it to tell the Wimp that a writable icon should only be able to accept certain characters, and any others will be rejected by the icon but passed instead through **Wimp_Poll** along with the unprocessed keys we mentioned above. An example will illustrate this. At the moment, our writable icon has block+28 (the address of a validation string if there is one) set to -1, indicating that no validation string is to be supplied, and that the writable icon defaults should be used when determining which characters to accept and which not. To make use of a validation string, dimension a small area of RAM at the start of the program and insert a short string as follows:

```
230 DIM valid% 20:$valid%="A~0-9"
```

Now alter the line which calls *FNcreate_icon* for the writable icon as follows:

```
280 i4handle%=FNcreate_icon(whandle%,8,-400,384,48,&7
00F13D,"",text1%,valid%,21)
```

You will see that we have replaced the -1 as the penultimate parameter with the address of our new buffer.

Now if you run the task again, everything will be as before, except that you will no longer be able to enter characters 0-9 from the keyboard. They will instead be passed to the task by **Wimp_Poll** reason code 8, and you will see the familiar message displayed each time you enter one of these characters.

The syntax for the validation string is somewhat involved. The first character in the string indicates what type of command is to follow, and in our string it is an "A", indicating a sequence of allowed characters. The tilde symbol "~" means the sequence which follows is disallowed. In our example we used "A~0-9". This is interpreted as *Allow all normal characters, except those in the range following the tilde.* To take another example, if you wanted to accept only upper case letters, the numbers 0-9 plus colons, full stops and commas, you would use "A0-9A-Z:.,". To allow only alphabetic characters and no others, you would use "AA-Za-z"

So far we have only looked at the A command within validation strings, but there are four others available in RISC OS 2:

D	the Display command
F	the Font command
L	the Line command
S	the Sprite name command

The D command can be used to conceal characters typed into an icon for use with passwords etc. The F command supplies colours for anti-aliased fonts, the L command tells the Wimp that a text icon may be formatted over a number of lines if it overflows the first, while the S command permits sprite names to be supplied for use with text and sprite icons. We shall be describing how to use sprites in icons in a moment. You can use more than one validation command in the same string by separating the commands with semicolons.

RISC OS 3 has a further three validation commands: R, which allows you to use fancy three dimensional icon borders; K, which enables you to specify actions for certain keys; and P, with which you can specify a sprite to be used for the pointer when over the icon.

A detailed description of validation strings is beyond the scope of this book, and you are recommended to read the information on **Wimp_CreateIcon** in the PRM if you wish to know more. But for the moment you might like to try one more example in *OurTask*. Alter line 230 to:

```
230 DIM valid% 20:$valid%="Aa-zA-Z;D\-"
```

This sets up the icon for password entry, accepting just upper and lower case alphabetic characters, but displaying them as dashes as you type.

SPRITE ICONS

So far all the icons we have created have been text only. But it is also possible to display sprites in icons, either on their own or with text as well. To do this, bit 1 of the icon flags must be set. If bit 0 is also set, it will be a text-plus-sprite icon, otherwise a sprite-only icon. Both kinds can be either indirected or non-indirected, though non-indirected text-plus-sprite icons are of little use since the sprite name and the icon text must be the same (since they both occupy the same space in the icon block).

Sprites used in icons can come either from the Wimp sprite pool, or from a sprite area set up by the program itself. The Wimp sprite pool contains all the sprites which are incorporated in the operating system ROM, together with any other sprites from sprite files which have been subject to an *IconSprites* command (see Appendix B). In other words, any sprite which is in a *!Sprites* file belonging to an application which has been seen by the Filer should be in the RAM area of the Wimp sprite pool.

When you use a sprite in an icon, the Wimp must be told where to find it. In the case of a non-indirected sprite icon, and also a text-plus-sprite indirected icon, the Wimp will look at the sprite area pointer for the window which contains the icon (at block+64 of the window parameter block - see Figure 2.3). If this is 1, the Wimp pool will be used, otherwise the pointer should point to a sprite area set up by the program. Appendix C gives details on setting up your own sprite area.

In the case of an indirected sprite-only icon, a pointer to a sprite area is provided at block+28 of the icon definition block, and this pointer overrides the pointer in the window block. This follows the same rules as before: 1 for the Wimp pool, or the specific address of a sprite area.

As for the name of the sprite, for a non-indirected icon this simply sits at block+24, just as icon text does for a text icon. If the icon is indirected, however, the location of the name depends on whether it is a sprite-only or a text-plus-sprite icon. In the former case, a pointer to the name is given at block+24, and the length of the buffer containing the name at block+32 (it is also possible to specify a pointer directly to the sprite definition itself, but for most purposes it is easier simply to use the name, as we shall do here). In the case of a text-plus sprite icon, the sprite name must be included in the validation string, prefaced by the S command.

To put all this into practice, we will add two further icons to *OurTask*. Add listing 5.4 to the program, and then run it. You should now see two more icons in the window, one of which displays a warning triangle, and the other a disc drive symbol.

Listing 5.4

```
  220 DIM text2% 10:$text2%="floppydisc"
  290 i5handle%=FNcreate_icon(whandle%,80,-492,88,88,&
1A,"error",0,0,0)
  300 i6handle%=FNcreate_icon(whandle%,220,-472,100,44
,&11A,"",text2%,1,11)
 1360 block%!64=1
```

Both the sprites we have used come from the ROM area of the Wimp sprite pool, so we have altered the window's sprite pointer to 1 in line 1360. Incidentally, to see the full range of sprites built into the ROM, run the following short program:

```
SYS "Wimp_BaseOfSprites" TO r%
SYS "OS_SpriteOp",268,r%,"ROMSprites"
```

which will save a sprite file called *ROMSprites*. Load this into Paint to see the sprites.

If you examine carefully what we have done here, you will see that icon 5 (the warning triangle) is a non-indirected sprite-only icon, with the sprite name "error", while icon 6 is an indirected sprite-only icon, with the sprite name "floppydisc" set up in *text2%* in line 220. You will see that the last three parameters supplied to *FNcreate_icon* are the pointer to the name buffer, the pointer to the Wimp sprite pool (1), and the length of the name buffer.

As a final example, we will create a set of radio icons using indirected text-plus-sprite icons. Our window is getting a little cluttered now, so we will remove all the other icons in the process. Add listing 5.5 to the existing program and then run it. You should now see a line of three radio icons, consisting of text alongside the familiar Acorn "radio button" sprites.

Listing 5.5

```
 210 DIM text1% 20,text2% 20,text3% 20
 220 $text1%="Fahrenheit":$text2%="Celsius":$text3%="Kelvin"
 230 DIM valid% 20:$valid%="Sradiooff,radioon"
 240 i0handle%=FNcreate_icon(whandle%,32,-100,240,44,&1722B113,"",text1%,valid%,21)
 250 i1handle%=FNcreate_icon(whandle%,32,-148,240,44,&1702B113,"",text2%,valid%,21)
 260 i2handle%=FNcreate_icon(whandle%,32,-196,240,44,&1702B113,"",text3%,valid%,21)
 270
 280
 290
 300
1510
1520
1530
1540
1550
1570
```

Let us now have a look at what we have done here. First of all, we have dimensioned three text buffers in line 210 to hold the text for the three icons, and placed the text into them in line 220. Next we have dimensioned a buffer at line 230 for the validation string, which in this case will hold the sprite name. Since all three icons use the same sprite, only one buffer is needed. In fact, *two* sprites are required, the first to represent the de-selected state of the icon, and the second for the selected state. The validation command allows us to do this by separating the two names with a comma, as we have done here: "Sradiooff,radioon". The initial "S" is the validation command, and the rest of the command tells the Wimp "use a sprite called "radiooff" when the icon is de-selected, and a sprite called "radioon" when it is selected". If you have already looked at the Wimp's ROM sprites as we suggested earlier, you will have seen that these two sprites are the Acorn radio button sprites.

The icons are created in much the same way as the others we have seen in this chapter, but the icon flags deserve a little explanation. When using text-plus-sprite icons, the state of the horizontal, vertical and right-justified flags determines where the text and the sprite appear relative to each other. For full details of this relationship you are referred to the PRM under the description of **Wimp_CreateIcon**. The normal configuration for radio icons with sprites is to set just the vertical bit (bit 4) which results in the sprite at the left with the text alongside it, as we have done here.

THE ICON BAR

We have almost finished our description of icons now, and although we have by no means exhausted the subject, a lot of information has been presented in this chapter. As we have said before, re-reading and experimenting is the best way to understand the complexities if you are still unsure about anything. Before we move on to menus, however, there is one further addition we can make to our program. One very noticeable thing about *OurTask* when compared to most other applications is that it does not install an icon on the icon bar, but starts up straight away by opening a window. We will now rectify this by making it behave in a more conventional fashion.

Installing an icon on the icon bar is very simple; all you have to do is create an icon using **Wimp_CreateIcon**, but specify the window handle as -1 (for the right-hand side of the icon bar) or -2 (for the left-hand side). The left-hand side of the icon bar is used for physical devices, such as printer drivers, disc drives etc., and the right-hand side for anything else.

The icon will normally be sprite-only, non-indirected, and the sprite you use will normally be the application's own sprite, i.e. the one which represents the application directory in a directory display. This sprite will already be in the Wimp sprite pool, since the application has to be seen before you can double-click on it. There are rules governing the positioning of icons on the icon bar; the Wimp will decide where to put them horizontally (because you will not know how many other icons there may be on the bar at the time), but the vertical position must be 0 (i.e. the icon bar's work area origin). The height should be 68 OS units (which equates to 17 pixels in mode 12), while the width can be any reasonable value, though if you are using an application sprite this will normally also be 68 OS units (34 pixels in mode 12). The button type for the icon flags will normally be 3 (click notifies task) since the whole purpose of having an icon on the bar is to respond to clicks from the user.

Finally, once the icon is installed on the bar, we no longer want the window to open when the task is started. This action can now be deferred until you click on the icon bar icon. As well as creating the icon in line 470, Listing 5.6

takes care of this by expanding *PROCclick* to differentiate between clicks over the window and clicks over the icon bar, and passing the latter to *PROCibar*. This procedure ascertains which button has been clicked (line 2210), and if it is Select or Adjust, the window is opened using the same commands as before (lines 2230-2250).

Listing 5.6

```
  30 REM Updated to Chapter 5
 440
 450
 460
 470 ibhandle%=FNcreate_icon(-1,0,0,68,68,&3002,"!ourtask",0,0,0)
 580
 590
 600 WHEN 6:PROCclick(block%!12)
1500 DEF PROCclick(win%)
1510 CASE win% OF
1520 WHEN -2:PROCibar(block%!8)
1530 WHEN whandle%:
1550 ENDCASE
2200 DEF PROCibar(button%)
2210 CASE button% OF
2230 WHEN 1,4:!block%=whandle%
2240 SYS "Wimp_GetWindowState",,block%
2250 block%!28=-1:SYS "Wimp_OpenWindow",,block%
2270 ENDCASE
2280 ENDPROC
2290 :
```

Now when you run *OurTask*, it will install its icon on the icon bar and wait for you to click on that icon with either Select or Adjust, whereupon the window will be opened as before. Note that the sprite *!ourtask* must exist, otherwise it will not appear on the icon bar (though the invisible icon itself will still be there and if you click on the space where the sprite should be, the window will still open). If you are not yet sure about creating application sprites, we would suggest that now is a good time to study Appendix B and create your *!ourtask* sprite.

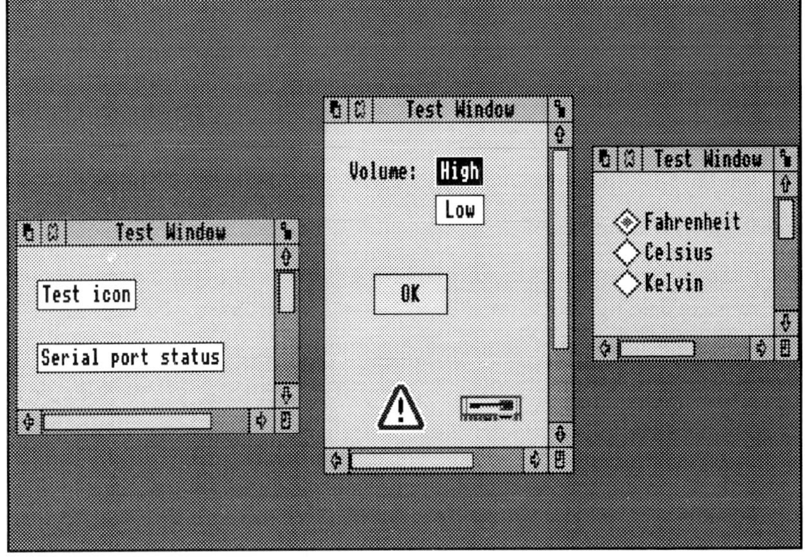

Figure 5.10
Icons created by the various listings in this chapter

In the next chapter we will describe menus in detail. In the meantime, Listing 5.7 below is the icon flag generator program referred to earlier.

Listing 5.7

```
   10 REM              >IconFlag
   20 REM Program    Icon Flag Generator
   30 REM Author     Lee Calcraft
   40 :
   80 MODE 12
   90 flag%=0
  100 PRINT"WIMP ICON FLAG GENERATOR"
  110 PRINT'"Generates 32-bit icon flag for use with Wi
 mp_CreateIcon"'
  120 INPUT "Default value (or Return) &"default$
  130 PRINT'"Respond with Y (=YES) Ret (=Copy) or any o
 ther key (=NO)"
```

```
 140 PRINT"to questions below about the window you are
creating"'
 150 IF default$="" THEN
 160 e%=FALSE
 170 ELSE d%=EVAL("&"+default$):e%=TRUE
 180 ENDIF
 190 REPEAT
 200 READ A%,A$
 210 IF A%<255 THEN
 220 IF e% THEN
 230 d$="N":IF (d% AND (1<<A%))>0 THEN d$="Y"
 240 ELSE d$=" "
 250 ENDIF
 260 PRINTA$;" (bit ";A%;")";TAB(55);d$;TAB(60)"Y/N ?
";
 270 B%=GET AND &DF
 280 IF B%=13 THEN
 290 B%=-(d$="Y")
 300 ELSE B%=-(B%=ASC"Y")
 310 ENDIF
 320 IF B%=1 THEN PRINT"Y" ELSE PRINT"N"
 330 flag%+=B%<<A%
 340 IF A%=6 THEN bit6%=B%
 350 ENDIF
 360 UNTIL A%=255
 370 PRINT'"The following options need decimal input (
or Return to copy)"
 380 READ A$,G%,B$
 390 shift%=0
 400 WHILE A$<>"Z" AND NOT(shift%=16 AND bit6%=1)
 410 shift%=VAL(LEFT$(A$,2))
 420 IF e% THEN
 430 de%=(d%>>>shift%)AND(2^G%-1)
 440 ELSE de%=0
 450 ENDIF
 460 PRINT B$;" (bits ";A$;")";TAB(55);de%;:INPUT TAB(
60);C$
 470 IF C$="" THEN
 480 C%=de%
 490 ELSE C%=VAL C$
 500 ENDIF
 510 flag%+=(C%<<shift%)
```

```
520 READ A$,G%,B$
530 ENDWHILE
540 PRINT'"Icon flag= &";~flag%
550 END
560 :
570 DATA 0,Contains text
580 DATA 1,Icon is a sprite
590 DATA 2,Icon has border
600 DATA 3,Horizontally centred
610 DATA 4,Vertically centred
620 DATA 5,Filled background
630 DATA 6,Text is anti-aliased
640 DATA 7,Needs task to redraw icon
650 DATA 8,Icon data is indirected
660 DATA 9,Text is right justified
670 DATA 10,If selected with Adjust keep ESG
680 DATA 11,Display sprite if any at half size
690 DATA 21,Icon (already) selected
700 DATA 22,Icon not selectable (shaded)
710 DATA 23,Icon has been deleted,255,
720 DATA 12-15,4,Icon button type
730 DATA 16-20,5,Exclusive selection group no
740 DATA 24-27,4,Foreground colour
750 DATA 28-31,4,Background colour,Z,0,Z
```

Chapter 6: Menus

The Wimp menu system - Creating a menu - Menu structure - Menu items - Menu icon flags and data - Menu positioning - Menu selection - Handling Adjust - Ticking and shading items - Submenus - Dialogue boxes - Implementing more than one menu

THE WIMP MENU SYSTEM

We come now to the last of the four major features of the Wimp system as expressed in the acronym itself. We have accounted for Windows, Icons and Pointers (the latter by implication since the actions of the mouse and pointer largely determine the behaviour of the rest of the system), and now it is finally the turn of menus.

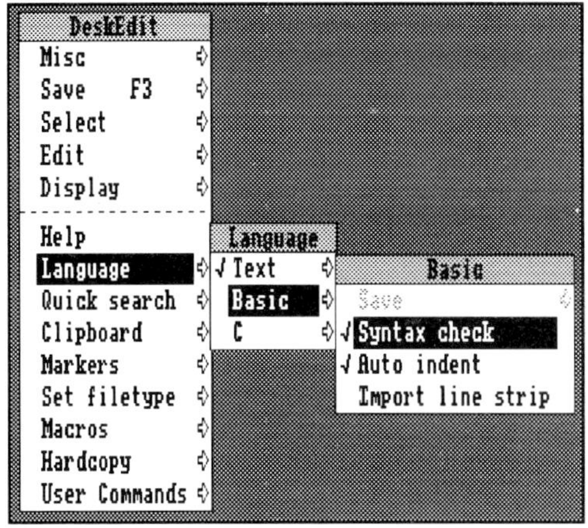

A typical Wimp menu structure

Menus are handled by the Archimedes Wimp in a manner consistent with other aspects of the system, and if you have understood the concepts introduced so far, what follows in this chapter should have a familiar feel to it. Menus are generated by calling the SWI **Wimp_CreateMenu** (&400D4). This call requires a large parameter block (mblock) to specify all the relevant data, including the text (or sprite) for each menu item, whether an entry is ticked, whether it has a right arrow indicating further options (or windows), the colours to be used and so on. Details of the parameters are shown in Figures 6.1a - 6.1c.

R1	=	pointer to menu block (see Figure 6.1b) or -1 to close any active menu
R2	=	x co-ordinate of top-left of top level menu (OS units)
R3	=	y co-ordinate of top-left of top level menu (OS units)

Figure 6.1a
Parameters for SWI
"Wimp_CreateMenu" (&400D4)

Menu block:

mblock+0	menu title (or null string)
12	title foreground and frame colour
13	title background colour
14	menu work area foreground colour
15	menu work area background colour
16	width of menu
20	height of each menu entry
24	vertical gap between items
28	menu items (24 bytes each) - see Figure 6.1c

Figure 6.1b
Menu block for Wimp_CreateMenu

Each menu item:

bytes 0-3 menu flags:

Bit	**Meaning when set**
0	display tick to left of item
1	dashed underline to separate item
2	item is writable
3	generate message when moving to submenu
7	this is last item in menu

all other bits must be zero

bytes 4-7	submenu pointer (>=&8000) or window handle (1-&7FFF) or -1 if none
bytes 8-11	menu icon flags (as for normal icon)
bytes 12-23	menu icon data (as for normal icon)

Figure 6.1c
Menu item data
(see text for variations in RISC OS 3)

Unlike the **Wimp_CreateWindow** call, which we described in Chapter 2, **Wimp_CreateMenu** actually puts the menu on the screen. The Wimp also handles the user's actions; for example, a click outside the menu area will remove the menu from the screen, while choosing an item from the menu will cause the Wimp to inform the task through **Wimp_Poll** reason code 9 (menu selection). The task can then just check the parameter block returned by the Wimp to find out which selection the user has made.

CREATING A MENU

The best way to see how the menu system works is to look at a real example. You will be aware by now that most applications which are installed on the icon bar have a menu which can be accessed by clicking the Menu button over the icon bar icon. Assuming that you have added the listings in the last chapter to *OurTask*, and the program therefore installs its icon on the icon bar, we can easily implement a simple menu.

Add Listing 6.1 to *OurTask*'s *!RunImage* program as before, and then run it. You will see that clicking Menu over the icon bar icon now displays a menu, albeit with only one item, *Quit*. However, selecting this item still has no effect - this is because we have not yet dealt with the program's response to the **Wimp_Poll** reason code which tells us that the selection has actually been made.

Listing 6.1

```
 160 DIM block% 255,imenu% 51
 440 RESTORE 20000:PROCsetupmenu(imenu%)
 860 DEF PROCsetupmenu(menu%)
 870 READ title$,num%:$menu%=title$
 880 width%=(LEN(title$)-2)*16
 890 menu%!12=&00070207:menu%!20=44:menu%!24=0
 900 ptr%=menu%+28:FOR i%=1 TO num%
 910 READ mflags%,subptr%,item$
 920 !ptr%=mflags%:ptr%!4=subptr%
 930 ptr%!8=&7000021:$(ptr%+12)=item$
 940 a%=(LEN(item$)+1)*16
 950 IF a%>width% width%=a%
 960 ptr%+=24:NEXT
 970 menu%!16=width%
 980 ENDPROC
 990 :
2260 WHEN 2:PROCshowmenu(imenu%,!block%-64,140)
```

```
 2400 DEF PROCshowmenu(menu%,mx%,my%)
 2470 SYS "Wimp_CreateMenu",,menu%,mx%,my%
 2480 ENDPROC
 2490 :
20000 DATA OurTask,1,&80,-1,Quit
```

Adding this listing has effectively made three major changes to the program. Firstly, a menu block is set up during the initialisation process by *PROCsetupmenu*. Secondly, *PROCibar* (which responds to button clicks over the icon bar icon) has now been extended to take account of clicks with Menu (line 2260). Thirdly *PROCshowmenu* has been added, which creates and displays the menu in response to such clicks. *PROCsetupmenu* in particular looks a little complex, but it has been designed as a general purpose procedure which can be called for each menu that needs to be set up. We will describe it in detail in a moment, but first we need to make a couple of comments about the parameter block used for this purpose.

We mentioned in the very first chapter of the book that there are some circumstances in which a parameter block for a SWI call requires a separate area of memory; i.e. you cannot use the same block that you are using for **Wimp_Poll** and all the other SWI calls we have discussed so far. The block required for **Wimp_CreateMenu** falls into this category. This is because the Wimp uses the information directly from the block to maintain the menu as long as it is displayed on the screen, so it must not be corrupted by any calls to **Wimp_Poll** or other SWIs which would occur between displaying the menu and processing a selection.

It would be quite possible to set aside one block specifically for menus (since you can only ever have one menu structure visible on the screen at any one time), and insert the data for the menu which is to be opened immediately before calling **Wimp_CreateMenu**. However, the approach we have adopted in our program is to set up a block containing the menu data as part of the initialisation process when the program is first run, and then whenever a menu is needed we simply pass the address of that block to *PROCshowmenu* which opens the menu by calling the SWI. This means, of course, that if we add further menu structures to our program (including any submenus) we must reserve a further block of memory for each one, but for the moment we only have one menu, for which we have reserved a block at *imenu%* (line 160). A menu block must be 28 bytes long plus 24 bytes for each menu item. Since we have only one item in our menu so far, we have therefore reserved a block of 52 bytes.

MENU STRUCTURE

PROCsetupmenu sets up the parameter block. We have written the procedure in such a way that it can be used as a general menu set-up procedure which takes its data from a DATA statement elsewhere in the program. This will allow you to alter the structure of the menu simply by altering the DATA statement, and to use the same procedure to set up further (and more complex) menus later.

The DATA statement contains first the menu title string, then the number of items in the menu. This is followed, for each item in turn, by its menu flags, submenu pointer and text. *PROCsetupmenu* reads the first two items, placing the title at the start of the block (line 870). Unlike icons or window title bars, a menu title cannot be indirected, and so must be no more than 12 characters in length. For a task's main menu, whether opened from the icon bar or from a window, the menu title would normally be the task name, and this is what we have done here.

Rather than specify the menu colours as single bytes, as we did when creating our window in Chapter 2, we have simplified the program and inserted just one hex value representing the four colours required at mblock+12 to mblock+15 (line 890). You should be proficient in understanding hex numbers by now, and so you will see from this that we have chosen black (colour 7) for the title foreground, grey (2) for the title background, black again for the work area foreground (i.e. the colour in which the menu item text will be displayed), and white (0) for the work area background. These are the standard recommended colours for menus and there is little point in altering them. Thus you can consider &00070207 (or just &70207) as a standard value to place in the block for all your menus.

The next three data words in the menu block relate to the general layout of the menu items. The menu width (mblock+16) determines how wide the Wimp draws the menu when it appears on the screen, in OS units. A sensible value for this is:

```
(maxlen%+1)*16
```

or:

```
(titlelen%-2)*16
```

whichever is the greater (where *maxlen%* is the length of the longest item in the menu, and *titlelen%* is the length of the menu title). The menu item height (mblock+20) is normally 44 OS units, and the vertical gap between items (mblock+24) is zero. It is not normally necessary to change these values. In *PROCsetupmenu* the width is calculated from the menu items as they are read in, and so must be inserted later. The height and gap, however, are put into the block at line 890.

MENU ITEMS

The menu item data shown in Figure 6.1c is largely self-explanatory. However, one or two things require a more detailed description. The word at bytes 4-7 is important, since it allows you to specify that a submenu should open up from that particular item. If the value of this word is greater than zero, the Wimp will automatically display an arrow to the right of the menu item, and with RISC OS 2 will treat the value as a window handle (if less than &8000) or a pointer to a further menu block (if &8000 or greater). Under RISC OS 3, window handles are simply pointers to the address in memory where the Wimp has stored the window definition, and so may be any 32-bit value. The Wimp itself will determine, from the structure pointed to, whether it is a window or submenu that needs to be opened.

The window or menu thus indicated will be displayed as a submenu whenever the pointer is moved across the arrow. In Listing 6.1 we have used a value of -1 to indicate that there is no submenu, but you can easily experiment by replacing this with the handle of our task's main window, as follows:

```
20000 DATA OurTask,1,&80,whandle%,Quit
```

Now if you run the program you will see an arrow to the right of the *Quit* option; moving the pointer across this displays the window we have seen before.

You will notice that in this case the window disappears as soon as the pointer is moved back onto the menu, or the mouse is clicked. This is because windows opened in this way behave exactly like menus in this respect. The ability to open windows in a menu structure allows the programmer to implement what are known as *dialogue boxes*. A dialogue box is a window which displays information and/or requests user input, usually opened as part of a menu and pertaining to the menu item from which it was opened. You can see a good example of a dialogue box by choosing the *Info* option which is available on the icon bar menu of most commercial applications, including Paint, Draw and Edit. In this case, the dialogue is one-way (i.e. no input from the user is required), but in the case of a save box (again, as implemented by most applications including the three mentioned above) the dialogue is two-way to allow the user to specify a filename.

If a menu item has a submenu, and if bit 3 of the menu flags is unset for that item, the Wimp will simply open the submenu or dialogue box without further ado whenever the pointer moves across the arrow. But if bit 3 is set, the Wimp will warn your task if this action occurs, using the Wimp messaging system which will be described in Chapter 8. This is useful if, for example, you want to calculate data before displaying it in the dialogue box, or to set the file icon in a save box to a particular filetype sprite before the box is opened. We will not be making use of this for the moment, but we will be covering it in Chapter 8, and the listing in that chapter will include an example of a submenu warning.

The other bits of the menu flags are self-explanatory. In *OurTask*, we do not want this particular item to be ticked, writable or followed by a line of dots, so bits 0-3 should be left as zero; however, our single item *is* the last item in the menu, which means that bit 7 must be set. This gives a value of &80 for the menu flags, and we have used this value in the DATA statement in line 20000.

MENU ICON FLAGS AND DATA

The icon flags and icon data have exactly the same format as for a standard icon, as described in the previous chapter (see Figures 5.4 and 5.6). However, not all the flags are now relevant. As we mentioned earlier in the book, the Wimp forces the button type of menu items (bits 12-15) to 9 (Menu icon). If the item is to be writable you should use the appropriate menu flag instead, as mentioned above. The ESG bits (bits 16-20) are also ignored, as are bits 4 (vertically centred) and 7 (requires task's help). Of the other bits, for a standard menu item you only need to set the colours (bits 24-31), a filled background (bit 5) and of course the text bit (bit 0). Assuming that you use the standard colours of black on white (which you should always do for the sake of uniformity), this results in a flags byte value of &7000021, which is what we have used at line 930. You would normally only deviate from this value in two circumstances: if the item's text is longer than 12 characters you would set the indirected bit (bit 8), giving a value of &7000121, and treat the item exactly as you would treat an indirected text icon; while if the menu item is to be shaded you would set the shaded bit (bit 22), which gives a value of &7400021.

Acorn's guidelines for menu items state that the first word should start with a capital letter, while subsequent words should be entirely in lower case. Thus your menu item would read "Save choices" rather than "Save Choices". Each item must also be left-justified, which is why we have left the horizontal formatting bits (bits 3 & 9) unset in the flags word. As we have said before, it makes a great deal of sense to follow the guidelines, since in a multi-tasking environment it is important that all applications have a common feel to the user.

MENU POSITIONING

Having set up the menu block at the start of the program as a permanent data structure, all that is needed to open the menu on screen is to call **Wimp_CreateMenu** with a pointer to the menu block in R1, and the required x and y co-ordinates of the menu in R2 and R3. This is achieved in our program by *PROCshowmenu* (lines 2400-2480) which takes as its three parameters the values required by R1-R3. *OurTask* has so far only set up an icon bar menu, so the procedure is called from *PROCibar* when a mouse click over the icon bar icon with the Menu button is detected.

The positioning of the menu requires a little elaboration. The menu should always be opened in relation to the position of the pointer, since it would make little sense for the user if the menu appeared at some distance from where the click was actually made. The x and y pointer co-ordinates can be read from block+0 and block+4 respectively when poll reason code 6 (mouse click) is returned. Acorn's guidelines cover the positioning of the menu in relation to these values. The left-hand edge should be 64 OS units to the left of the pointer, while the vertical position depends on whether it is an icon bar menu or not. If it is, then the bottom of the menu must be 96 OS units from the bottom of the screen. If it is not, the bottom edge of the menu title bar should align with the pointer.

In practice, this means that a menu should normally be opened with a horizontal position of !block-64, while a menu which is not opened from the icon bar icon should have a vertical position of block!4. For an icon bar menu, provided you have used the standard menu item height and gap of 44 and 0 respectively, the value for the vertical position will be 140 for a single-item menu (i.e. 96+44), with 44 added for each subsequent item (plus an additional 24 units for any dotted line between items). If you look at line 2260 of Listing 6.1, you will see that we have indeed passed values of *!block%*-64 and 140 to *PROCshowmenu*.

MENU SELECTION

We will expand our menu structure later in the chapter, but before any menu can be of use to the task, some method must be provided to decode selections made by the user. To do this, we need to insert an additional line into the Wimp poll CASE statement to respond to reason code 9. In *OurTask*, we have only one menu with only one item, *Quit*, so we know for certain that if this reason code is ever returned, it means the user wishes to quit. Thus we can simply add the following line to our program:

```
630 WHEN 9:quit%=TRUE
```

Now when you run the program, you will find that choosing the *Quit* option from the menu terminates the task.

In the majority of cases, however, it is not as simple as this. In practice, a program may have more than one menu structure, and each menu will normally have more than one item, with the possibility of submenu items as well. To decode the correct selection, we must make use of the information supplied by the Wimp. The actual parameter block returned with reason code 9 is as follows:

block+0 item in main menu which was selected (starting from 0)
block+4 item in first submenu which was selected
block+8 item in second submenu which was selected
and so on

This list is terminated by a word containing the value -1; for example, if the item selected is in the first submenu, then the word at block+8 would be -1.

To see this in practice, we will expand our menu to include a few more items, and instead of simply quitting when a selection is made, we will add a procedure to decode it and perform the appropriate action. Add Listing 6.2 to the *OurTask* program and then run the program. You will now see that as well as the *Quit* option, there are three further options: *Fahrenheit*, *Celsius* and *Kelvin*. Try opening the program's window and see the effect of choosing one of these extra options.

Listing 6.2

```
  160 DIM block% 255,imenu% 123
  630 WHEN 9:PROCmenuselect
 2260 WHEN 2:PROCshowmenu(imenu%,!block%-64,272)
 2500 DEF PROCmenuselect
 2510 sel1%=!block%
 2550 CASE sel1% OF
 2560 WHEN 0,1,2:FOR i%=0 TO 2
 2570 !block%=whandle%:block%!4=i%
 2580 IF i%=sel1% block%!8=&200000 ELSE block%!8=0
 2590 block%!12=&200000
 2600 SYS "Wimp_SetIconState",,block%
 2610 NEXT
 2620 WHEN 3:quit%=TRUE
 2760 ENDCASE
 2780 ENDPROC
 2790 :
20000 DATA OurTask,4,0,-1,Fahrenheit,0,-1,Celsius,0,
-1,Kelvin,&80,-1,Quit
```

We have added the additional menu items by expanding the DATA statement at line 20000, not forgetting at the same time to increase the size of the reserved block at line 160, and to alter the vertical position of the menu in line 2260.

The rest of the additions to the program consist of our decoding routine. Firstly, we have now altered line 630 so that our response to reason code 9 is to call *PROCmenuselect*. Since our menu only has one level, we are only interested in the value at block+0, and a variable *sel1%* is set up to hold this value. A simple CASE statement is used to determine the action to be taken as a result of the selection. If the value is 0, 1 or 2 (i.e. one of the first three items on the menu), the corresponding radio icon in the window is selected, and the others deselected. This is done by using **Wimp_SetIconState**, which we described in Chapter 5 (refer to Figure 5.8 and the accompanying text if you are not clear about the process involved). The loop beginning at line 2560 cycles through the three icons. In line 2580 the selected bit (bit 21) in the Clear word is set if the icon number corresponds to the menu selection, and zero if it does not. By setting the bit in the EOR word in both cases, the bit in the icon flags will now be set by the call to **Wimp_SetIconState** for the corresponding icon, and cleared for the other two.

If the value of *sel1%* is 3, this means the *Quit* option has been chosen, and *quit%* is set to true as before.

HANDLING ADJUST

It is a RISC OS convention that clicking with the Adjust button on a menu entry should have the same effect as Select, except that the menu tree should be kept open. This is obviously a useful convention, since you often need to make a number of consecutive selections from a menu, and it would be very tiresome if the whole menu tree always disappeared with each selection.

To make a menu system perform in this way is easy. All you need to do is to use SWI **Wimp_GetPointerInfo** (&400CF) each time a menu selection is reported to the task via poll reason code 9. Figure 6.2 gives details of the block returned by this call.

block+0	mouse x
4	mouse y
8	button state
12	window handle (-1 = background, -2 = icon bar)
16	icon handle

Figure 6.2
Block returned by SWI "Wimp_GetPointerInfo" (&400CF)

By using **Wimp_GetPointerInfo** you can read the button state to see if the user made the selection with Select or Adjust. If Adjust was used, then all you have to do is call **Wimp_CreateMenu** before returning to the poll loop. This causes the Wimp to re-open the menu tree at the same place, and in such a way that it appears never to have been closed. Of course, if the user's selection necessitates a change in the menu data (such as placing a tick against an item, which we will look at later), the data must be updated before calling **Wimp_CreateMenu** or the new state of the menu will not be apparent on the screen. To handle the Adjust button in *OurTask*, all you need to do is add Listing 6.3. You will now find when you run the program that choosing a menu option with Adjust will have the same effect as with Select, but the menu will stay on the screen.

Listing 6.3

```
2520 SYS "Wimp_GetPointerInfo",,block%
2530 button%=block%!8
2770 IF button%=1 PROCshowmenu(imenu%,0,0)
```

Lines 2520-2530 call **Wimp_GetPointerInfo** and read the button state from block+8 into *button%*. Then in line 2770, after the selection has been decoded, *button%* is evaluated and if it is 1 (meaning Adjust was pressed), *PROCshowmenu* is called. The menu co-ordinates are irrelevant this time, since the Wimp will recognise this as the menu which is currently open anyway, and will re-open it in exactly the same place.

TICKING AND SHADING ITEMS

When using RISC OS applications, you may have noticed that sometimes a menu item is accompanied by a tick at the left-hand side, while at other times it is shaded. The reasons for doing this are entirely up to the task, but normally a tick is used to indicate that a particular option is one which is currently in force, while a shaded item is an option which cannot currently be selected (and the Wimp reinforces this, since a shaded icon cannot be selected by the user anyway). The very existence of ticked and shaded items implies that these may change during the course of using the program, and so if you are using a permanent menu block as we have done here, it is necessary to modify the data in the block before calling **Wimp_CreateMenu** to take account of any changes that may have been made to the status of the items.

In the *OurTask* program as it currently stands, it would be logical for the menu to reflect the current state of the radio icons by ticking the corresponding menu item. Adding Listing 6.4 will implement this.

Listing 6.4

```
 170 quit%=FALSE:app$="OurTask":iconsel%=0
1530 WHEN whandle%:iconsel%=block%!16
2420 FOR i%=0 TO 2
2430 a%=imenu%+28+i%*24
2440 IF i%=iconsel% THEN ?a%=(?a% OR 1) ELSE ?a%=(?a%
AND 254)
2450 NEXT
2610 NEXT:iconsel%=sel1%
```

We have now introduced a variable *iconsel%* which holds the number of the currently selected icon of the three in the radio group. A click over one of these icons now sets this variable to the icon number (in *PROCclick* at line 1530), as does choosing the appropriate option from the menu (in *PROCmenuselect* at line 2610). When the menu is actually displayed by *PROCshowmenu*, lines 2420-2450 cycle through the icons. Line 2430 calculates the position in the menu block of the menu flags for each icon; then if it is currently selected, line 2440 sets bit 1 of the menu flags to mark it as ticked, while if it is deselected the same line unsets the bit. If you now run the program, you will see that the ticked option always corresponds to the currently selected radio icon, whether it is altered from the menu or by clicking on the icon itself. If you use Adjust to make the menu selection, you will see that any change in the position of the tick is reflected immediately.

SUBMENUS

As we have already mentioned, any Wimp menu can have submenus, indicated by an arrow to the right of a menu entry, and these may themselves have submenus and so on. There is in fact a SWI call **Wimp_CreateSubMenu,** but this is usually only used if the programmer requires the task to intervene in some way when a submenu is accessed by the user, as we indicated earlier. We will look more closely at this call in Chapter 8 when we consider the submenu warning message. Normally, however, the whole menu system, complete with its submenus, is created by placing a suitable data block in memory for each menu and submenu, and then calling **Wimp_CreateMenu** in response to the user clicking Menu at the appropriate place. Provided that we have inserted the address of each submenu's data block into the menu data of the associated entry in the parent menu or submenu, the Wimp will handle the whole job for us.

To see how this works we will implement a single submenu by removing the three additional options from the main menu and placing them into a submenu, accessed by an entry in the main menu entitled "Scale". Adding Listing 6.5 to the current version of the program will achieve this. The result is shown in Figure 6.3.

Listing 6.5

```
  160 DIM block% 255,imenu% 75,smenu% 99
  450 RESTORE 20010:PROCsetupmenu(smenu%)
  570
 2260 WHEN 2:PROCshowmenu(imenu%,!block%-64,184)
 2430 a%=smenu%+28+i%*24
 2510 sel1%=!block%:sel2%=block%!4
 2560 WHEN 0:IF sel2%<>-1 THEN
 2565 FOR i%=0 TO 2
 2580 block%!8=-&200000*(i%=sel2%)
 2610 NEXT:iconsel%=sel2%
 2615 ENDIF
 2620 WHEN 1:quit%=TRUE
20000 DATA OurTask,2,0,smenu%,Scale,&80,-1,Quit
20010 DATA Scale,3,0,-1,Fahrenheit,0,-1,Celsius,&80,
-1,Kelvin
```

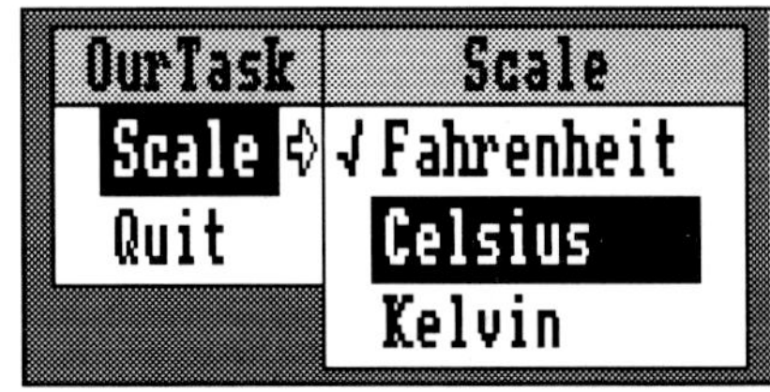

Figure 6.3
A submenu implemented by Listing 6.5

The first thing we must do is reserve a fresh area of memory for the submenu block; this results in *smenu%* being dimensioned at line 160. Next the submenu block is set up by calling *PROCsetupmenu* again in line 450, with the data pointer at a new DATA statement in line 20010. When the menu is displayed, the calculation of the position of the tick now relates to *smenu%* and not *imenu%* as before, and this is taken care of in line 2430. The majority of the changes that we have made affect *PROCmenuselect*. Firstly, we must now set up a new variable *sel2%* to hold the value of any selection made from the submenu. Then the main CASE statement must be altered to reflect the fact that there are now only two choices on the main menu. If *sel1%* is zero, this means that the selection was made from option 0 on the main menu, but this could occur both if *Scale* was chosen directly from the main menu, or if one of the submenu options was chosen. In the former case, block+4 (and hence *sel2%*) will hold -1, while in the latter case it will hold the number of the option chosen. To ensure that the user has in fact clicked on a valid submenu item, we have included the IF...ENDIF construct at lines 2560 and 2615 so that the icons are only altered if *sel2%* does not hold -1.

In this particular example, choosing any of the submenu options will activate the same process, namely setting the state of the icons. Normally a submenu would contain a set of options each of which requires a separate action on being selected. This is easily catered for by arranging the structure of *PROCmenuselect* as a series of nested CASE statements. For example, if your main menu had two options as above, and the first item led to a submenu with three options, the structure of the procedure would look something like this:

```
sel1%=!block%:sel2%=block%!4
CASE sel1% OF
 WHEN 0:CASE sel2% OF
  WHEN 0:
  WHEN 1:
  WHEN 2:
 ENDCASE
 WHEN 1:
ENDCASE
```

DIALOGUE BOXES

We suggested earlier as a brief experiment that you could place the handle of *OurTask*'s main window into the menu block to simulate a dialogue box. Listing 6.6, when added to the existing program, creates a more conventional dialogue box: a standard Info box similar to those used by most commercial applications (see Figure 6.4). To do this, we need to create a second window, and this requires some amendments to *FNcreate_window*. We need to add two further parameters when calling the function: the window flags and the title.

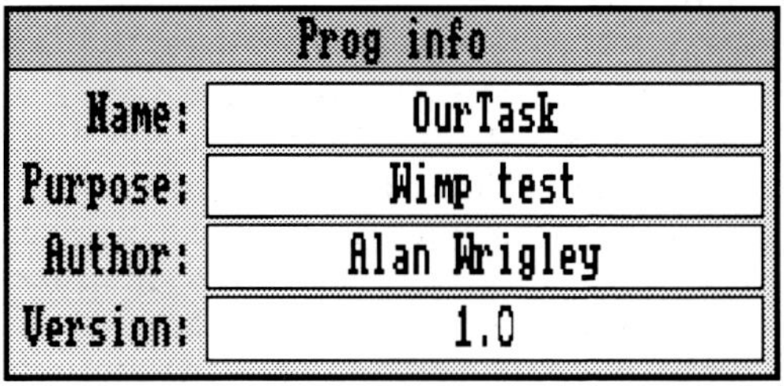

Figure 6.4
Dialogue box produced by Listing 6.6

Listing 6.6

```
  30 REM Updated to Chapter 6
 160 DIM block% 255,imenu% 99,smenu% 99
 200 whandle%=FNcreate_window(200,200,300,500,200,20
,&FF000012,"Test window")
 270 info%=FNcreate_window(0,0,580,204,0,0,&84000012
,"Prog info")
 280 RESTORE 15000
 290 FOR i%=1 TO 4:READ text$
 300 a%=FNcreate_icon(info%,0,-i%*48-4,144,44,&17000
211,text$,0,0,0)
 310 NEXT
 320 FOR i%=1 TO 4:READ text$
 330 a%=FNcreate_icon(info%,148,-i%*48-4,424,44,&700
003D,text$,0,0,0)
 340 NEXT
1000 DEF FNcreate_window(x%,y%,w%,h%,extx%,exty%,fla
gs%,title$)
1140 block%!28=flags%
1400 $(block%+72)=title$
2260 WHEN 2:PROCshowmenu(imenu%,!block%-64,228)
2560 WHEN 1:IF sel2%<>-1 THEN
2620 WHEN 2:quit%=TRUE
15000 DATA Name:,Purpose:,Author:,Version:
15010 DATA OurTask,Wimp test,Alan Wrigley,1.0
20000 DATA OurTask,3,0,info%,Info,0,smenu%,Scale,&80,
-1,Quit
```

Line 270 creates a new window, and lines 280-340 fill it with the required icons. This is done in two groups; those down the left-hand side ("Name", "Purpose" etc.) in the loop from lines 290-310, and the rest in the second loop (lines 320-340). You should be able to work out the characteristics of each group of icons by studying the values of the icon flags. Finally, a third option, *Info*, is added to the main menu and the handle of the info box is supplied in the menu block. The info box will now appear whenever the pointer moves across the arrow from the main menu option. You will notice that while the info box is on the screen, you can drag it around with the mouse. This is because our task is responding to poll reason code 2 (open window request) using the window handle returned by the Wimp, which in this case will be the info box handle.

IMPLEMENTING MORE THAN ONE MENU

So far we have only created one menu structure, based on the icon bar. But most tasks have at least two menu structures; it is quite common for a click with Menu over a task's window to produce a different menu from that which appears over the icon bar icon. This is quite simple to achieve - all you need to do is create a separate data block containing the data for the second menu structure, and use the address of this instead as a parameter when calling *PROCshowmenu*. However, there is one important point to take into account: as far as the Wimp is concerned, you have simply asked it to open a menu, and it has no idea whether this is your only menu or one of several. This means that you must keep a record of which menu is opened, since otherwise when the menu selection is returned through **Wimp_Poll**, *PROCmenuselect* will not know from which menu the selection has been made.

The simplest way to do this is to set a variable (for example *menuopen%*) to a different value for each menu when it is opened, and read this variable at the start of *PROCmenuselect*. Since each menu has a separate data block in memory, we can use this as the value for *menuopen%*, safe in the knowledge that the value will be unique to that menu structure. An extra line in *PROCshowmenu* will set this up:

```
2410 menuopen%=menu%
```

So if *PROCshowmenu* is called from the icon bar, *menuopen%* will have the same value as *imenu%*, while if it is called from a window it will have the same value as the block which defines the window menu (perhaps *wmenu%*). Having done this, you then need to add a further CASE statement to *PROCmenuselect* at the top level:

```
2540 CASE menuopen% OF
2550 WHEN imenu%:CASE sel1% OF
```

Incidentally, don't be tempted to leave out line 2410 and use *menu%* directly as the value of the open menu. This will not work, since *menu%*, being a parameter of *PROCshowmenu*, is local to that procedure and will therefore have a value of 0 if used elsewhere. You must set a global variable to the value as we have done above with *menuopen%*.

We have now covered all the basic elements in a Wimp program, and our acronym is complete. You should find by now that the concepts we are describing are easier to understand, as you get used to the way in which the Wimp works. If not, do please re-read this chapter, and if necessary previous chapters, before you go on. The techniques we have covered so far are quite adequate to enable you to construct your own simple programs, and it is worth taking a short break at this point to see whether you can design and program a useful application for yourself in order to gain some experience in using the Wimp. We have not yet covered the loading and saving of data, but there are many useful functions which could be performed by using the basic techniques. For example, you could design a currency converter which takes a value from the user via a writable icon, and converts it into one of a range of foreign currencies, selectable from a group of radio icons, or from a menu perhaps.

You should be able to think of many similar examples of applications which can easily be implemented by windows, icons and menus. Now is the time to start playing around with these ideas, which can then be built on as we cover the more advanced aspects of Wimp programming in the rest of this book.

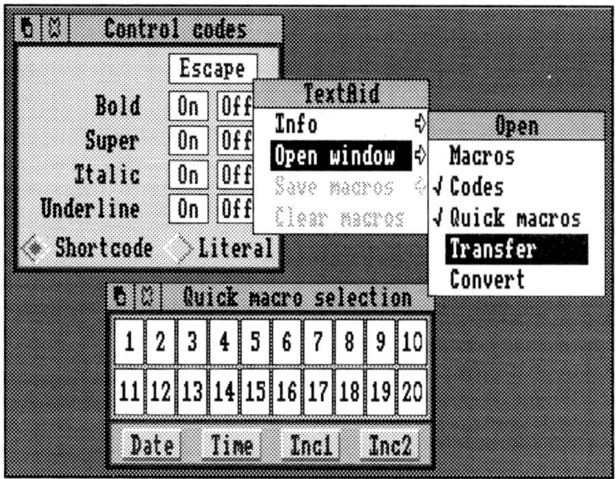

The main elements of a Wimp application - windows, icons and menus

7. Redrawing Windows

Introduction to user-redraw - The redraw process - Example program - Forcing a redraw - Efficient redraws - Redrawing text - Redrawing text held in an array - Redrawing graphics

INTRODUCTION TO USER-REDRAW

In the program listings introduced so far in this book, we have made the assumption that all displays of information in the program's windows can be achieved by using icons. When this is the case, the Wimp can usually redraw any window on the screen without any help from the task itself. However, there are many applications which would find it impossible or inappropriate to use icons to display certain information. For example, it would be very laborious for Edit to handle an ever-changing screen full of text by using writable icons, while Draw would find it impossible to display even the simplest picture without the ability to draw it directly onto the window as a graphic object.

In fact, we have already hinted in Chapter 2 that it is possible to do just that, when we described window flag 4 (Wimp needs no help from task to redraw window), and again in Chapter 3 when we said that poll reason code 1 (redraw request) would only be returned by the Wimp if that flag was unset. We also said that the redrawing of the window must be carried out in a special way, and in this chapter we will show you how to do this. There is quite a lot of detail and theory involved, so as usual we recommend that you re-read any sections that are unclear, and also experiment as much as possible with the program.

THE REDRAW PROCESS

We have seen that when **Wimp_Poll** returns a reason code of 2 this constitutes a request by the Wimp to open (or re-open) a particular window. This occurs when you click on the Adjust size icon or the title bar of a window, when the window is dragged around, or when scroll bars are moved to a new position. The usual way for the task to respond to this is to call **Wimp_OpenWindow**, just as we have done in line 550 of *OurTask*. This puts the onus back on the Wimp to manage any redrawing of the window which is necessary.

In response to our call to **Wimp_OpenWindow**, the Wimp will begin the business of opening (or re-opening) the nominated window. During this process it checks window flag 4 (see Figure 2.8), and if this is set, it puts the window on the screen. Many windows, however, will have bit 4 unset, meaning that the task must be invoked to draw text or graphics in the window. In such cases, if the user's action results in a previously obscured part of the window becoming visible, the Wimp will immediately return a reason code of 1 (redraw window request) to the task, and the task must respond to this in a special way. It cannot simply respond by directly drawing text or graphics onto the screen; the window in question might still be partly obscured by another.

What the task must do is to put into operation a well-defined process, and this must be done immediately; it must not make any other Wimp calls until it has serviced the redraw request in the correct manner. First of all the task must call **Wimp_RedrawWindow** (&400C8), and then repeatedly call **Wimp_GetRectangle** (&400CA) until the Wimp tells it that no more parts of the window need updating. Details of the parameter block returned by both these calls are given in Figure 7.1.

R0=0	No more updating required
R0>0	Further updating required

R1 points to a parameter block:

block+0	Window handle
4	Visible area minimum x co-ordinate
8	Visible area minimum y co-ordinate
12	Visible area maximum x co-ordinate
16	Visible area maximum y co-ordinate
20	Scroll x offset relative to work area origin
24	Scroll y offset relative to work area origin
28	Current graphics window minimum x co-ordinate
32	Current graphics window minimum y co-ordinate
36	Current graphics window maximum x co-ordinate
40	Current graphics window maximum y co-ordinate

Figure 7.1
Information returned by
SWI "Wimp_RedrawWindow" (&400C8) and
SWI "Wimp_GetRectangle" (&400CA)

The first seven parameters returned in the block (block+0 to block+24) are fairly self-explanatory. However, the last four parameters, the co-ordinates of the current graphics window, need further explanation. When the call to **Wimp_RedrawWindow** is made, the Wimp decides which parts of the window need redrawing. This could be the whole window, but if it is partially covered by other windows, it could be a series of rectangles which, taken together, add up to the total area on display (see Figure 7.2). So the Wimp returns the co-ordinates of each of these rectangles in turn until there are no more to be updated. These co-ordinates make up the current graphics window detailed in Figure 7.1.

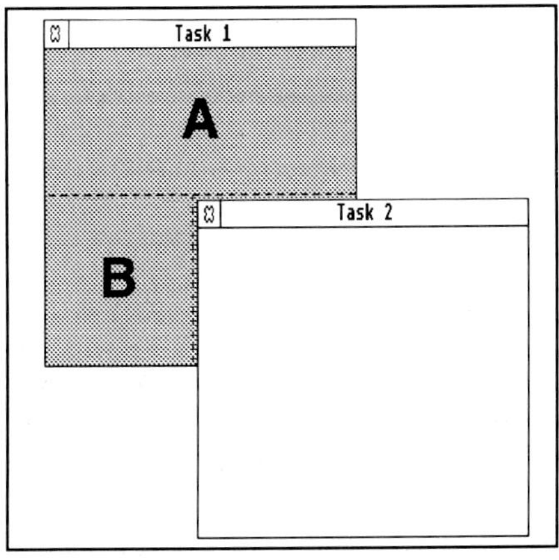

Figure 7.2
Window Updating.
If the Wimp needs to update Task 1, it will split the area into rectangles A and B, and request in turn that each of the two be updated

Each time the Wimp returns a rectangle for updating, it sets a clipping window to the perimeter of the rectangle, clears the area to the background colour (unless the window's work area has been set to transparent - see Figure 2.3), and issues a VDU 5 command (write text at the graphics cursor). Finally it fills the parameter block, and returns the task a flag in R0. If this is non-zero it indicates that the parameter block contains a rectangle to be updated, while if it is zero this means that there is no more updating to be done, and the redraw loop can be terminated.

The task in its turn redraws that area with whatever text or graphics it requires, and then (provided that the flag is not zero) calls **Wimp_GetRectangle**, which sets up the next rectangle in the sequence. This continues (with a whole series of calls to **Wimp_GetRectangle**) until all the rectangles in the window which had become invalid have been updated, and the job is complete. If you look carefully as you use the Desktop you can often see this process in action. For example, if you have a complex drawing displayed in a Draw window, and you remove a window or menu tree which previously obscured all or part of it, the Wimp will update the Draw window bit by bit.

Thus the whole redraw process will be accomplished by a segment of code which looks something like this:

```
SYS "Wimp_RedrawWindow",,block% TO flag%
WHILE flag%
REM do the actual updating here
SYS "Wimp_GetRectangle",,block% TO flag%
ENDWHILE
```

In practice, a task can respond in two different ways to the parameter block returned. The simplest way is to redraw everything in the whole of the window's work area when the first rectangle is requested. This relies on the clipping window to ensure that only those parts of the window which the Wimp requires will actually be drawn on screen. Of course, if you have a very large work area (as you might with a text editor full of text for example) this approach would be impossibly slow, since the task would need to write the whole text file to the screen every time the Wimp needed to update even a square centimetre.

A much more efficient (and more complex) approach is for the task to narrow down the contents of the work area as closely as possible to the actual segment of window which the Wimp is updating with each rectangle, and draw this part only (bearing in mind of course, that if you are dealing with sprites it is not feasible to split them). Initially we will adopt the former approach in *OurTask* for simplicity, but later in the chapter we will look more closely at how to keep the redrawing process fast and efficient.

EXAMPLE PROGRAM

Add Listing 7.1 to your existing *!RunImage* program and run the OurTask application. The window will now be a little larger, and alongside the group of three radio icons you will now see a vertical coloured bar. The top half of this bar should be red, and the bottom half pale blue. On the right-hand side of the bar you should see three figures displayed: 212 at the top of the bar, 32 at the junction between red and blue, and -523 at the bottom. The window display produced is shown in Figure 7.3.

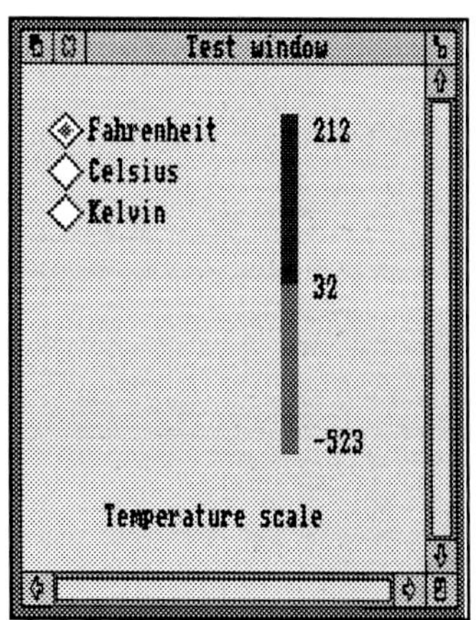

Figure 7.3
Window produced by Listing 7.1

Incidentally, having added this listing, we suggest you keep a copy of the program in its current state, since we will be returning to it in Chapter 9.

Listing 7.1

```
  160 DIM block% 255,imenu% 99,smenu% 99,limits%(2,2)
  200 whandle%=FNcreate_window(200,200,500,600,0,0,&F
F000002,"Test window")
  350 FOR i%=0 TO 2:FOR j%=0 TO 2
  360 READ limits%(i%,j%):NEXT:NEXT
  530 WHEN 1:PROCredraw
 2800 DEF PROCredraw
 2810 SYS "Wimp_RedrawWindow",,block% TO more%
 2820 ox%=block%!4-block%!20
 2830 oy%=block%!16-block%!24
 2840 WHILE more%
 2850 PROCdraw(ox%,oy%)
 2860 SYS "Wimp_GetRectangle",,block% TO more%
 2870 ENDWHILE
 2880 ENDPROC
 2890 :
 2900 DEF PROCdraw(x%,y%)
 2910 SYS "Wimp_SetColour",11
 2920 RECTANGLE FILL x%+320,y%-260,20,200
 2930 SYS "Wimp_SetColour",15
 2940 RECTANGLE FILL x%+320,y%-460,20,200
 2950 SYS "Wimp_SetColour",7
 2960 MOVE x%+360,y%-64
 2970 PRINT;limits%(iconsel%,2)
 2980 MOVE x%+360,y%-248
 2990 PRINT;limits%(iconsel%,1)
 3000 MOVE x%+360,y%-432
 3010 PRINT;limits%(iconsel%,0)
 3020 MOVE x%+100,y%-520
 3030 PRINT"Temperature scale"
 3080 ENDPROC
15020 DATA -523,32,212,-273,0,100,0,273,373
```

As you may have guessed, the figures represent the values in the selected temperature scale for boiling point, freezing point and absolute zero respectively. The values for all three scales are set up in an array *limits%* in lines 350-360.

Line 530 adds a statement to the poll loop to respond to reason code 1 (the window flags having been altered by the amendment to line 200 such that flag 4 - Wimp needs no help to redraw - is now unset). The response is to call *PROCredraw*, which contains the redraw loop almost exactly as we described earlier. The program uses lines 2820-2830 to work out exactly where on the screen our window is to be displayed, and then every time the Wimp asks for a segment of it to be redrawn, it redraws the lot using *PROCdraw*, relying on the clipping window set up by the Wimp to ensure that only the nominated rectangle is updated each time.

Working out the origin for the redraw is performed very simply in lines 2820 and 2830, but explaining the calculation is a little less simple. Figure 7.4 shows the relationship between visible area, work area and scroll offsets. Essentially, the Wimp parameter block available to us contains the visible area minimum and maximum x and y co-ordinates, and the scroll offsets (as well as information on the co-ordinates of the rectangle within the window which needs updating, but we are ignoring these since we are redrawing the whole window anyway). We need to calculate the work area minimum x and y co-ordinates in terms of the graphics origin. Getting the x co-ordinate is easy: we just subtract the scroll offset from the visible area minimum x co-ordinate. For the vertical dimension we take the maximum visible area y co-ordinate and subtract the vertical scroll offset (which itself is measured downwards, and will therefore be negative).

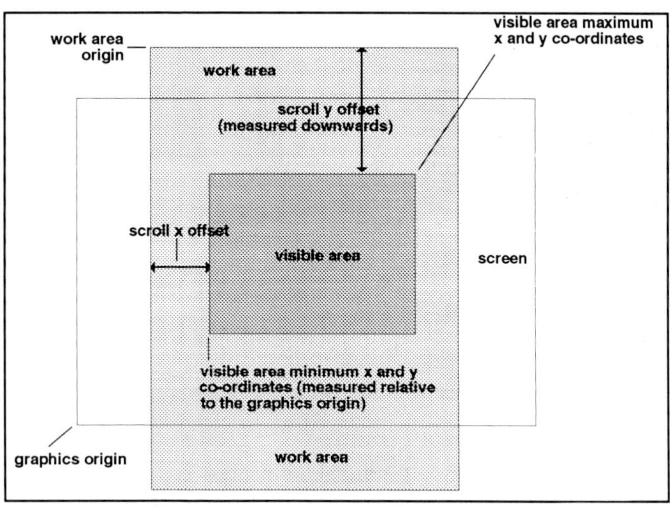

Figure 7.4
Calculating the origin for window redrawing

With this under our belt we can go about the business of writing to our window, and this is accomplished by *PROCdraw*. First of all the two sections of the vertical bar are drawn, using the RECTANGLE FILL command for each (lines 2920 and 2940). In order to set the colour we wish to use, we have introduced another SWI call, **Wimp_SetColour** (&400E6). This serves to define the current graphics colour. We cannot simply use GCOL for this purpose because this would give a colour dependent upon the currently set mode, and multi-tasking programs should wherever possible work in all modes. The parameter supplied with the call is simply the colour number (0-15) in the Wimp palette. To get an idea of the range of colours available, take a close look at the Desktop palette icon. This contains all 16 colours displayed in numerical order from 0 at the top left to 15 at the bottom right.

Having drawn the vertical bar, we now print the values alongside it. All text printing under the Wimp is done in VDU 5 mode; i.e. text is written at the current graphics cursor. For this reason, we need the three MOVE statements in lines 2960, 2980 and 3000 to enable us to print the figures in the correct place. Finally a further MOVE/PRINT pair of statements writes a legend across the bottom of the window (lines 3020-3030). Note the way we have subtracted from the y co-ordinate in all cases, since the work area origin is at the top of the window, and all y values within the window must therefore be negative.

The values printed in the window are calculated by reading the elements of the array *limits%* which relate to the current value of *iconsel%*. You can see that this is so by closing the window and selecting one of the other two temperature scales from the icon bar menu, then re-opening the window. The values will now have changed to those of the scale you have chosen. However, you will notice that if you change scale by clicking on one of the radio icons, nothing happens to the window display. This is because the redrawing of the window is only done in response to requests from the Wimp to do so - and this will only happen if the window is closed and then re-opened, or if part or all of it becomes visible after being obscured. Try altering the scale by clicking on an icon, and then drag another window across *OurTask*'s window. The values displayed will now be the correct ones for the chosen scale, because the Wimp has asked for the window to be updated.

It would be inconvenient to have to close and re-open a window, or drag others over it, just to update information in this way, and so a call exists which will force the Wimp to issue a redraw request at any time if necessary. We will look at this in just a moment, but first it is worth experimenting with *PROCdraw*. Try altering the colours and positions of the items, and writing your own text in line 3030. If you replace the string in the listing with a piece of text more than 25 characters long you will discover that the right-hand end of it is irretrievably lost. Text does not automatically drop down on to the next line as it does when printing to a single-tasking screen in VDU 4 mode.

In other words, if you are using the Wimp, you cannot get text onto the screen by simply executing a series of PRINT statements. You need to go about the whole process with a great deal of care. We have already seen that each PRINT statement must be preceded by a MOVE statement, and the length of each line of text must be less than the width of the work area.

Moreover, if you have an application which generates some text as its output, you cannot always PRINT this to the screen the moment that the information becomes available, because you must have a way to refresh as much of the screen as the Wimp requires whenever the Wimp requests it. Thus if you are writing a Cross Referencer say, which displays the names of functions and procedures in a program file which has been dragged to it, you must actually write your findings to a buffer area in RAM within the task program rather than printing them in the first instance; you must then implement a routine to display the contents of the buffer whenever a redraw request is received. Clearly you cannot implement a new search for procedures or whatever each and every time the Wimp needs to redraw the display. This problem will of course occur in applications of many different kinds, and its resolution will add a level of complexity to all such programs.

FORCING A REDRAW

Under normal circumstances the initiative for redrawing a window comes from the Wimp itself, as we have seen so far in this chapter. This will occur when a previously closed window is opened, or an obscured part becomes visible, perhaps because the user has scrolled it or moved another window aside. However, there will be many cases where the task needs to initiate an update. For example, a clock may need updating every second or minute, or a character may have been typed into a text editor, or a database search routine may have found a matching string. *OurTask* already provides a perfect example: when the temperature scale is altered by clicking on an icon in the window, the values displayed alongside the vertical bar will need changing. In such cases (as always) the task must not write directly to the window, since it might be partially, or even wholly, obscured. It must instead force the Wimp to perform the updating, and there are two ways in which this may be achieved:

1. Call **Wimp_ForceRedraw** (SWI &400D1), supplying the area to be updated. This causes the marked area to be registered as invalid. The Wimp will then in due course set about its renewal - probably by returning a redraw window request at the next Wimp poll.

2. Call **Wimp_UpdateWindow** (SWI &400C9), supplying the area to be updated. In this case, the Wimp immediately initiates the redraw, returning the co-ordinates of the first rectangle to be redrawn by the task. The task should comply, and repeatedly call **Wimp_GetRectangle** until the Wimp signals that there are no more sections which need updating.

In other words, calling **Wimp_ForceRedraw** tells the Wimp "I want to redraw this part of my window at the earliest possible opportunity; please issue a redraw request". This means that the window will actually be redrawn later as part of the normal redraw routine in response to poll reason code 1. On the other hand, calling **Wimp_UpdateWindow** is saying "I am redrawing this window *now*; please return all the necessary rectangles for me to complete the job".

Both approaches are similar, but the latter gives immediate results because the window updating does not have to wait for all other concurrent tasks to make their next call to **Wimp_Poll**. The other difference is that in the latter case, the Wimp does not clear each rectangle before its co-ordinates are passed to the task for updating. This can be particularly useful when moving objects across a display using EOR plotting logic, such as when using rubber banding techniques.

The second method uses more code, however, and is really only worth considering if you need the background to remain uncleared, so for the purposes of *OurTask* we will opt for the first method. In this case, all you need to do is to make a single call to **Wimp_ForceRedraw** with the following data in registers R0-R4:

R0 = window handle (-1 means whole screen)
R1 = minimum x co-ordinate of area to redraw
R2 = minimum y co-ordinate of area to redraw
R3 = maximum x co-ordinate of area to redraw
R4 = maximum y co-ordinate of area to redraw

As you may infer from this, the call can be made in one of two ways: you can set R0 to -1, in which case the co-ordinates refer to the screen origin, or better still you can set R0 to the handle of the window to be updated, in which case the co-ordinates refer to the work area of the window. Listing 7.2 adopts the latter approach, and all that is needed is to add two lines, which cause a forced redraw each time one of the three radio icons is clicked or the appropriate menu item is chosen. Incidentally, it is worth repeating at this point our recommendation in the first chapter that you should list the whole program section when adding lines to *!RunImage*, in order to understand more fully the purpose and context of the new lines.

Listing 7.2

```
1540 SYS "Wimp_ForceRedraw",whandle%,360,-460,440,-56
2612 SYS "Wimp_ForceRedraw",whandle%,360,-460,440,-56
```

Figure 7.5 shows the relationship between the last four parameters supplied to **Wimp_ForceRedraw**. There are two important points to note in supplying the parameters for this call. Firstly, although the measurements are made relative to the work area origin, the first of the two vertical parameters (minimum y) is numerically larger, and it is very easy to reverse accidentally the order in which they are given. Secondly, because all measurements are made relative to the work area origin (which is usually at the top of the work area), both maximum and minimum y will always be either zero or negative.

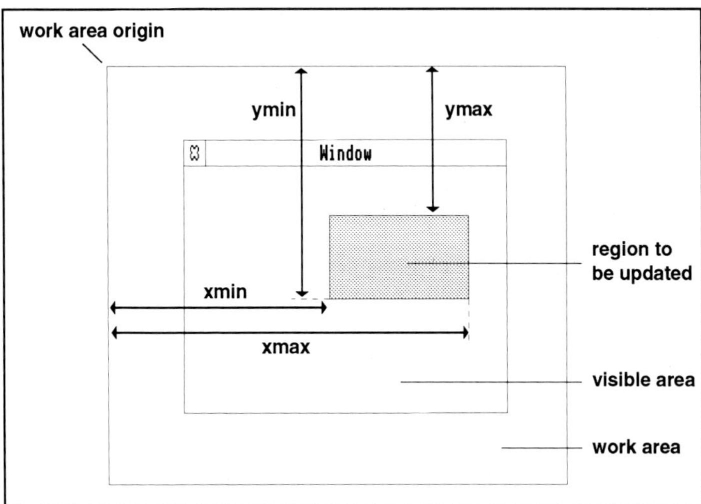

Figure 7.5
The relationship between the work area origin and the region to be updated in a forced redraw

Incidentally, it is worth mentioning at this point that as well as using this call to redraw the window's contents, you would also use it to alter the window title (provided that the title has been indirected). For example, you may have noticed that most applications which edit text or graphics display an asterisk after the title shown in the title bar when the data has been modified but not saved. This is standard RISC OS practice, and allows the user to see at a glance if the data in the window is safe or not. To do this, the application will create the window with an indirected title string. When the asterisk needs to be added or removed, the title bar string will be updated in the buffer and then the task will force a redraw of that part of the window which covers the title bar.

EFFICIENT REDRAWS

Even in this simple example, you may be able to glimpse some of the problems involved in updating a window. We have only updated one simple rectangle, which has the same co-ordinates each time. But imagine a digital clock displaying hours, minutes and seconds plus the day and date. This will require updating once every second, but for the most efficient redraw only those parts which have actually changed should be updated. This means that the rectangle may include just the seconds display, or the seconds and minutes, and so on up to the full display if the clock is still running when midnight comes around. This requires constant recalculation of the rectangle to ensure that the redraw takes the minimum possible time to complete on each occasion.

As an even more complex example, imagine that the work area contains large quantities of editable text. As soon as the user types a single character at the keyboard, the window must be updated, and if the cursor is somewhere in the middle of a document the ramifications from a single keypress can be enormous. All text beyond the cursor may need to be rewritten, and this can be a lengthy business, even in machine code. In many cases (a DTP document for example) the text will be displayed in an outline font rather than the system font, and this will make matters very much worse.

To see how fast an application can respond to redraw requests, load a large text file into Edit, and then move a small window across it. You will see that redrawing is handled quite efficiently, and the progress of the window which you are dragging is not noticeably slowed - unless the text in Edit contains very long lines (or worst of all, no linefeeds at all). In this case, redraw is impossibly slow.

It takes more than a little thought to ensure that your Wimp task contains fast and effective redraw routines. The simplest way to achieve great speed would be to let the Wimp do all the work, and put all your text into icons. This sort of approach is only suitable for very specific applications however. It is impractical for large quantities of text, or text that is to be manipulated to any degree. In such cases you will have to resort to writing your own fast redraw routine. We will give you some guidelines on the best ways to do this.

REDRAWING TEXT

The principle involved in creating fast text redraw routines is simple: redraw only that part of the window which the Wimp nominates. In practice you can get away with redrawing complete lines of text (of up to 40 or even 80 characters in length), provided that you only redraw those lines which fall within the nominated area. This makes life a bit easier, since we only need to worry about the y co-ordinates of the redraw rectangle.

Exactly what form the code in your redraw loop will take depends on how you have stored the text which is to appear in your window. Perhaps the simplest approach is to store it in some form of array, for example a simple string array in which each line of the display is held in a separate element. This is easy to handle, and we will look at this case first, but before doing so we will mention a more flexible alternative.

If you have a sizeable quantity of text in your work area, and especially if you are to manipulate it in any way, then long string arrays are out, since they provide no flexibility at all. The only viable alternative is to store the text directly in memory, perhaps using character 13 as an end of line marker, or perhaps without any such markers. In either case, you must hold an array of pointers to the start of each line. This is essential, because there is no time to work through the whole file to discover where each line begins once a redraw request has been received. The redraw process is extremely time critical, and if it is slowed down in any way the Desktop will become very sluggish indeed.

By holding an array of pointers you can immediately find the start of the line of text to be displayed, given the number of the line, counting from the start of the text file. We will give an example of this technique in due course, but we will start with the slightly simpler case of text held in a string array.

REDRAWING TEXT HELD IN AN ARRAY

The best way to see how this is achieved is to look at an example. Listing 7.3 when added to *OurTask* implements a fast redrawing routine, and one whose speed is independent of the amount of text held. The procedure assumes that the text to be redrawn is held in the array *display$*, and that there are currently *dispsize%* valid lines.

Listing 7.3

```
  200 whandle%=FNcreate_window(200,200,800,600,400,140
 0,&FF000002,"Test window")
  240
  250
  260
  370 PROCmakearray
 1530
 1540
 2612
 2842 top%=(oy%-block%!40) DIV 32
 2844 IF top%<0 top%=0
 2846 base%=(47+oy%-block%!32) DIV 32
 2848 i%=top%
 2850 WHILE i%<dispsize% AND i%<=base%
 2852 MOVE ox%,oy%-(i%<<5)
 2854 PRINT display$(i%)
 2856 i%+=1
 2858 ENDWHILE
 2900 DEF PROCmakearray
 2910 DIM display$(200):j%=1
 2920 a$=STRING$(8,"Wimp Test ")
 2930 FOR i%=0 TO 200
 2940 display$(i%)=MID$(a$,j%,60)
 2950 j%=j% MOD 10+1
 2960 NEXT
 2970 dispsize%=i%
 2980
 2990
 3000
 3010
 3020
 3030
```

PROCmakearray (called in line 370 when the program is initialised) sets up a suitable text array. The response to poll reason code 1 in line 530 is now diverted to a new procedure, *PROCredraw2*, which forms a straighforward redraw loop, designed to display the block of text indented by 16 OS units from the left hand side of the window. First of all we obtain the co-ordinates (in OS units) of the work area origin by subtracting the position of the x and y scroll bars from the co-ordinates of the top left-hand corner of the visible area. All this information is returned by the call to **Wimp_RedrawWindow**, as we saw in Figure 7.1.

As you can see from the program there are two nested WHILE loops. The outer one cycles round once for each rectangle which the Wimp requests to be redrawn, while the inner one prints just those lines which feature in the nominated rectangle. This is achieved by obtaining values for *top%* and *base%*. These are the upper and lower bounds of the region that the Wimp has requested to be redrawn, and are measured in OS units relative to the work area origin. To determine which lines of the array we need to print we just divide these values by 32 (since each line of text is 32 OS units in height regardless of which mode is used in the Desktop). At the bottom end (*base%*) we add a small measure to counteract the effect of rounding down (since integer division is used), and that's all there is to it.

The case where the text to be written is held in a block of memory is very similar. Suppose that the array *array%* contained a set of pointers to the start of each line of text in such a way that *array%*(0) contained the address of the start of the first line of text, and so on. All we would need to do to alter *PROCredraw* appropriately is to replace the PRINT statement in line 2854 by:

```
2854 PRINT $array%(i%)
```

This assumes that each line of text is terminated by a carriage return character in memory.

Incidentally, to see just how slowly the redraw routine operates when the whole text file is redrawn in response to every redraw request, alter the assignments of *top%* and *base%* in the outer WHILE loop of *PROCredraw* as follows:

```
2842 top%=1
2846 base%=dispsize%
```

If you now re-run the program you will see that any attempt to drag an object across the task's window is very slow - and this is only with a very short text file.

REDRAWING GRAPHICS

When redrawing graphics objects, two different approaches can be adopted. Either you can use a technique similar to that discussed above for use with text, where you determine the co-ordinates of the area to be redrawn and redraw just that area; or you can take a short-cut and use sprites. In practice, the first of these two methods may not be feasible in all situations. It may not be possible to draw the right-hand part of a graphic without having drawn the left-hand part first - or at least without having calculated where the left-hand part would fall. Also there may be no easy way to know exactly which part of your drawing code to activate to draw a particular segment of a drawing.

For example, suppose the graphic is a map of the UK, and that it is drawn from an array of points. There is no obvious way to get from the bounding rectangle returned by the Wimp with a redraw request to co-ordinates of the points required to redraw the nominated area. In such cases, the fastest redraw will often be obtained by initially creating a sprite covering the graphic area, drawing the graphic when it needs to be altered by directing VDU output to the sprite, and then plotting the sprite on the screen when redraw requests are made. Of course large sprites can take up a great deal of memory, but this method can be very effective. For those readers who are interested in pursuing this, Listing 7.4, when added to *OurTask*, will create a sprite containing a simple graphic (see Figure 7.6), and this will be plotted in response to the Wimp's redraw requests.

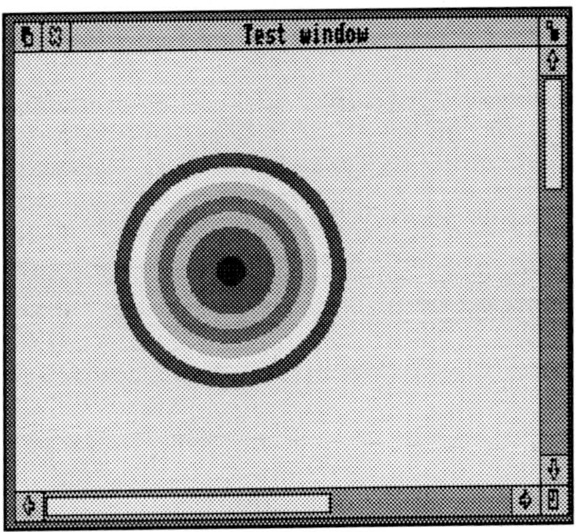

Figure 7.6
Sprite created by Listing 7.4 and plotted onto the window during the redraw loop

Before running the program after the addition of this listing, you will probably need to increase the WimpSlot allocation in the *!Run* file from 32K to 64K, as the program requires quite a bit of extra memory to store the sprite. Otherwise you may find that when you run the program, you get an error such as "No room for this DIM".

Listing 7.4

```
  30 REM Updated to Chapter 7
 370 PROCmakesprite
1530 WHEN whandle%:PROCdrawsprite
1540 SYS "Wimp_ForceRedraw",whandle%,100,-500,500,-10
0
2842
2844
2846
2848
2850 SYS "OS_SpriteOp",&122,sparea%,"test",ox%+100,oy
%-500,0
2852
2854
2856
2858
2900 DEF PROCmakesprite
2910 SYS "OS_ReadModeVariable",-1,4 TO ,,xeig%
2920 SYS "OS_ReadModeVariable",-1,5 TO ,,yeig%
2930 xsize%=400>>xeig%:ysize%=400>>yeig%
2940 DIM sparea% xsize%*ysize%
2950 !sparea%=xsize%*ysize%:sparea%!8=16
2960 SYS "OS_SpriteOp",&109,sparea%
2970 SYS "OS_SpriteOp",&10F,sparea%,"test",0,xsize%,y
size%,MODE
2980 SYS "OS_SpriteOp",&118,sparea%,"test"
2990 PROCdrawsprite
3100 DEF PROCdrawsprite
3110 SYS "OS_SpriteOp",&13C,sparea%,"test",1 TO r0%,r
1%,r2%,r3%
3120 SYS "Wimp_SetColour",1
3130 RECTANGLE FILL 0,0,400
3140 FOR i%=8 TO 1 STEP -1
3150 SYS "Wimp_SetColour",RND(7)+8
3160 CIRCLE FILL 200,200,i%*20
3170 NEXT
3180 SYS "OS_SpriteOp",r0%,r1%,r2%,r3%
3190 ENDPROC
3195 :
```

PROCmakesprite is called at line 370 during the initialisation process, and creates the sprite. For a full description of **OS_ReadModeVariable** and **OS_SpriteOp**, you should refer to the PRM, but briefly what is happening is as follows: firstly, lines 2910 and 2920 read the pixel-to-co-ordinate ratio for the current mode. This ensures that the sprite appears to be the same size whatever screen mode is in use. A sprite area is set up in lines 2940-2960, and a sprite called "test", 400 x 400 OS units large, is created at line 2970 and selected at line 2980. *PROCdrawsprite* is then called, which switches VDU output to the sprite at line 3110, ready for drawing a set of concentric randomly coloured circles which is done in lines 3140-3170. Finally, line 3180 restores VDU output to its previous setting.

Lines 1530-1540 of *PROCclick* have now been altered so that when a mouse button is clicked over the window, *PROCdrawsprite* is called again, resulting in a new set of circles being drawn onto the sprite. Line 1540 forces a redraw of the area of the window containing the sprite.

When *PROCredraw* is called from the poll loop, all it now has to do is to plot the sprite onto the window (line 2850). And that's all there is to it. This is a very simple example, but you should be able to see how to adapt this for your own purposes if you want to display complex graphics in a window.

If you find the subject of redrawing windows rather complicated, it is worth persevering, and experimenting with the program listings, since there are a great many applications where it is preferable by far to use this method of displaying information in a window, rather than having to rely on icons to do all the work.

8. The Wimp Message System, Loading and Saving Data

The message system - Receiving messages - Message action codes - File information utility - Error-returning SWI calls - Data transfer protocol - Sending messages - Implementing a save box - Object dragging - Saving data - Submenu warnings

THE MESSAGE SYSTEM

The message system is a very important part of the Wimp, and is the primary means by which two or more tasks communicate with each other. This includes communication with the Filer when file icons are dragged to or from directory viewers, and so all loading and saving of files which is carried out in this way must be controlled through the message system. There are many more uses for the message system than this, however, and the section on the relevant SWI call is one of the longest in the PRM. In the course of this chapter we will look at all of the most common uses for Wimp messages, though we would recommend that you read the PRM for a complete description. As usual, there is a great deal of detail to be mastered in this chapter, and we make no apologies for repeating our exhortation to re-read anything which at first appears unclear.

RECEIVING MESSAGES

A task can send a message by using the SWI **Wimp_SendMessage** (&400E7). Messages are received in turn through **Wimp_Poll**, using reason codes 17-19 (see Figure 3.2 in Chapter 3). We will look in detail at the reception of messages first, since all tasks should respond to at least one message from the Wimp, whether they send any themselves or not.

The precise difference between the three reason codes used by the Wimp for messages will be explained later. For the moment we can safely ignore reason code 19, and so our poll loop only needs to respond to reason codes 17 & 18. For most tasks these may be bracketed together and passed through the same routine, as in the following example:

```
WHEN 17,18:PROCreceive
```

MESSAGE ACTION CODES

When a message is sent or received, a parameter block is used to convey all the necessary information accompanying the message. The format of this is shown in Figure 8.1. When receiving a message, the first thing a task has to extract from this block is the *action code* (block+16). This is set up by the sender and is used to relay the purpose of the message to the recipient, for example, a mode change or a request to load a data file. The RISC OS 2 PRM documents 20 or so action codes, and most tasks will only be interested in these. The RISC OS 3 PRM has information on many more, and some commercial applications may generate their own action codes, either for private use or for the benefit of other software which can respond to them.

block+0	size of block in bytes (max 256)
4	task handle of message sender
8	*my_ref* - the sender's reference for this message
12	*your_ref* - a previous message's *my_ref*, or 0 if not a reply
16	message action code
20	message data - the format of this depends on the action code at block+16

Figure 8.1
Wimp message parameter block

As we indicated earlier, every task must respond to at least one type of message, which is *Message_Quit* (action code 0). There are usually three main methods of quitting an application. Firstly, you can choose the task's *Quit* menu option (if it has one). Secondly, you can open the Task Manager's *Tasks* window (see Figure 8.2), click Menu over the task name and choose *Quit* from the *Task* submenu. And thirdly, you can shut down the whole Desktop by pressing Ctrl-Shift-F12. With the first method, the task itself will decode the instruction to quit and perform the necessary action. In the second case, the Wimp will send the task a *Message_Quit*, while in the third case the Wimp will broadcast the message to all active tasks. If this message is received, the task must shut down immediately.

If you run *OurTask* in its present incarnation, then open the *Tasks* window, you will see the name *OurTask* listed in the top section of the window. Click Menu over the name, move across to the *Task* submenu and choose the *Quit* option. You will see that nothing happens, since we are not responding to any messages from the Wimp. Now add listing 8.1 to *!RunImage* and repeat the process. This time the task should terminate when you click on the *Quit* option, and its name will be removed from the list of active tasks.

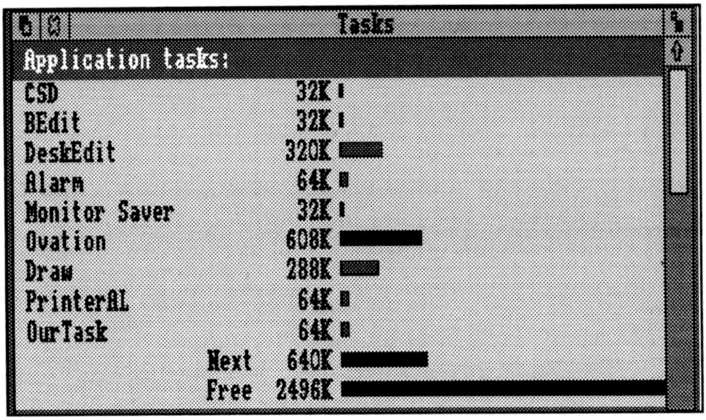

Tasks
Application tasks:
CSD 32K
BEdit 32K
DeskEdit 320K
Alarm 64K
Monitor Saver 32K
Ovation 608K
Draw 288K
PrinterAL 64K
OurTask 64K
Next 640K
Free 2496K

Figure 8.2
Part of the Task Manager's Tasks *window*

Listing 8.1

```
 650 WHEN 17,18:PROCreceive
3200 DEF PROCreceive
3210 CASE block%!16 OF
3220 WHEN 0:quit%=TRUE
3270 ENDCASE
3280 ENDPROC
3290 :
```

In this particular case the structure of *PROCreceive* is very simple. A CASE statement decodes the message action code from block+16, and since we are only responding at present to action code 0, only one WHEN statement is required (line 3220).

Figure 8.3 shows some of the more useful action codes and their names, and we will consider how and why these are used. We said just now that if a task receives a *Message_Quit*, it must terminate immediately, i.e. without delaying or making any further calls to the Wimp. But suppose the task has unsaved data; if it were to shut down immediately in this way the data would be lost. So before the *Message_Quit* is sent, the Wimp sends a *Message_PreQuit* (action code 8). The task must acknowledge this message (by sending a message back, as we shall describe later in the chapter), and is then free to prompt the user to save data or whatever before terminating.

0	Message_Quit
1	Message_DataSave
2	Message_DataSaveAck
3	Message_DataLoad
4	Message_DataLoadAck
8	Message_PreQuit
&400C0	Message_MenuWarning
&400C1	Message_ModeChange

Figure 8.3
Some useful message action codes

Message_MenuWarning (action code &400C0) is sent by the Wimp to a task if the user moves the pointer across a submenu arrow on a menu tree, provided that bit 3 of the menu flags is set for that item, as we described in Chapter 6. The purpose of this is to enable the task to carry out some processing before the submenu is actually opened; this might involve updating some information in a dialogue box, for example. We will include an example of this in *OurTask* shortly.

Message_ModeChange (action code &400C1) is broadcast by the Wimp if the screen mode has been changed by the user, perhaps by choosing a new mode from the palette menu. Many programs (*OurTask* included) do not need to worry about this, but it could be that some applications need to make an assumption about the number of characters on the screen or some other mode-dependent variable. If this is the case, then on receipt of this message they will be able to update any relevant data by reading the state of the variables for the current mode.

Message action codes 1-4 are all part of the data transfer protocol, and as such form a vital part of the multi-tasking process in the Archimedes. The ability to transfer files from application to application, and to and from the Filer by dragging, is one of the factors that make the RISC OS Desktop so powerful. Later in the chapter we will be looking more closely at the data transfer protocol, and using it to implement a save box routine for *OurTask*. We will also have more to say at that point about the *my_ref* and *your_ref* fields in the message parameter block (refer back to Figure 8.1). For the moment, however, you can get a brief taste of how part of the protocol works by adding Listing 8.2. If you now run the updated program and drag any object to it from a directory display, a beep will sound. The pitch of the beep will be different depending on whether the object dragged is a file, a directory or an application.

Listing 8.2

```
 370
1520 WHEN -2:IF block%!8=2 PROCibar(block%!8)
1530
1540
3240 WHEN 3:PROCdataload(block%!40)
3300 DEF PROCdataload(type%)
3310 CASE type% OF
3320 WHEN &1000:SOUND 1,-10,80,4
3330 WHEN &2000:SOUND 1,-10,120,4
3340 OTHERWISE:SOUND 1,-10,200,4
3350 ENDCASE
3480 ENDPROC
3490 :
```

What is happening here is that the Filer is informing our task via *Message_DataLoad* (action code 3) that a drag has been performed whose destination is one of the icons or windows owned by our task. The information returned with this message is shown in Figure 8.4. If the action code is 3, *PROCdataload* is called at line 3240. This reads the filetype from block+40 (see Figure 8.4); this will be a three-digit hex number for a file, &1000 for a directory and &2000 for an application. The program generates a sound which is different for each of these three object types. Incidentally, you will notice that the effect is the same whether you drag the object to *OurTask*'s icon bar icon or into its window. This is because we have made no attempt to read the window or icon handle of the drag's destination point from the parameter block; all we have concerned ourselves with is the fact that the drag has ended at a point on the Desktop which in one way or another belongs to our task.

block+20	destination window handle
24	destination icon handle
28	destination x co-ordinate
32	destination y co-ordinate
36	estimated size of data in bytes
40	filetype
44	full pathname of file, zero-terminated

Figure 8.4
Data block returned with **Message_DataLoad**
(action code 3)

FILE INFORMATION UTILITY

There are a good many practical uses for this facility. Being able to drag files to an application's icon or window is a vital part of the functionality of RISC OS. Once the drag has been signalled, the task can do what it likes with the object which has been dragged, which may involve loading it, processing it, renaming it or whatever. Sounding a beep, as our task does at present, is not particularly useful (though it does prove the program is responding correctly) so we will expand the function of the application a little by adding Listing 8.3 to the *!RunImage* program. When this has been done, running the application will provide a file information utility. Dragging any object to the icon bar icon will open a window showing the object type (file, directory or application), the full pathname of the object, and the filetype both as a hex value and in its textual form (see Figure 8.5). If you were unaware that filetypes had a textual description associated with them, press F12 to get to the command line and then type:

```
Show File$Type*
```

You will see a list of system variables of the form *File$Type_nnn* each followed by a text string, where *nnn* represents the hex value of a filetype and the string is the text label belonging to that type.

Because *OurTask* now performs a useful practical function, it is worth studying the whole program carefully to see how all the various elements of a working Wimp program fit together.

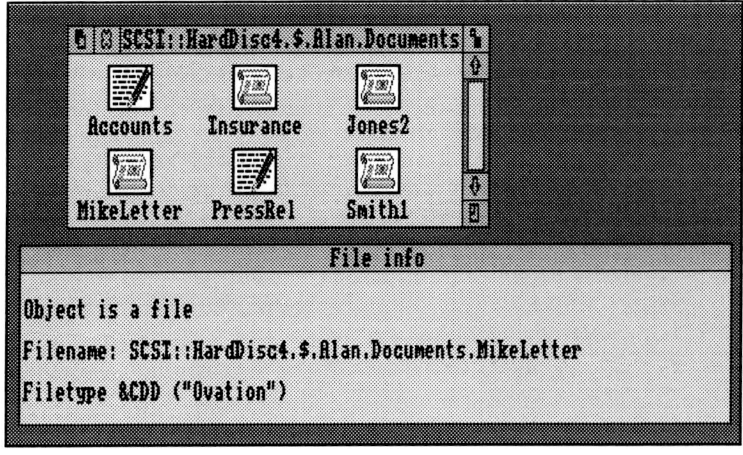

Figure 8.5
File information utility produced by Listing 8.3.
The file "MikeLetter" has just been dragged to the icon bar icon

Listing 8.3

```
   200 whandle%=FNcreate_window(100,300,1080,220,0,0,&
84000002,"File info")
   210 path$="":type$="":obj$=""
   220 desc$="Object is a"
   370
   450
  1520 WHEN -2:PROCibar(block%!8)
  2260 WHEN 2:PROCshowmenu(imenu%,!block%-64,184)

  Delete 2560-2615

  2620 WHEN 1:quit%=TRUE
  2845 MOVE ox%+4,oy%-40:PRINT obj$
  2850 MOVE ox%+4,oy%-100:PRINT "Filename: "+path$
  2855 MOVE ox%+4,oy%-160:PRINT "Filetype: &"+type$

  Delete 2900-3195

  3320 WHEN &1000:obj$=" directory"
  3330 WHEN &2000:obj$="n application"
  3340 OTHERWISE:obj$=" file"
  3360 path$=FNstring(block%+44)
  3370 type$=STR$~type%
  3380 SYS "XOS_ReadVarVal","File$Type_"+type$,block%,
255,0,3 TO ,,len%
  3390 block%?len%=13:type$+=" ("""+$block%+""")"
  3400 obj$=desc$+obj$
  3410 !block%=whandle%
  3420 SYS “Wimp_GetWindowState”,,block%
  3430 IF block%!32 AND 1<<16 SYS “Wimp_ForceRedraw”,w
handle%,0,-220,1080,0
  3440 block%!28=-1:SYS "Wimp_OpenWindow",,block%
  3500 DEF FNstring(ptr%)
  3510 LOCAL a$
  3520 WHILE ?ptr%<>0
  3530 a$+=CHR$(?ptr%):ptr%+=1
  3540 ENDWHILE
  3550 =a$
  3560 :
 20000 DATA OurTask,2,0,info%,Info,&80,-1,Quit
 20010
```

There are some important points that need to be covered in this listing. Firstly, you may remember that in Chapter 4 we said that many strings returned by SWI calls were terminated with a zero byte, and that a function would be described to convert these into strings readable by Basic's string-handling functions (i.e. they must be terminated by a carriage return). We now need that function, since as we have seen from Figure 8.4, the pathname returned in the message block is zero-terminated. *FNstring* (lines 3500-3550) performs the conversion, taking the address of the zero-terminated string as a parameter and adding characters onto an output string one at a time until a zero byte is found. As the output string is a standard Basic string, it will automatically be terminated by a carriage return.

Lines 3320-3340 in *PROCdataload* determine whether the object is a file, directory or application as before, but now all that happens at this point is that *obj$* is set up to contain a string describing one of these types as appropriate; this will eventually be added to *desc$* (defined in line 220) to form part of the display in the window. Line 3360 sets up *path$* to hold the pathname obtained from the message block via *FNstring*, while at line 3370 *type$* holds a string representing the hex value of the filetype. Line 3380 introduces a SWI call which we have not met so far, **OS_ReadVarVal**. This is not a Wimp call, and so you are referred to the PRM for full details, but it is a very useful call which reads the value of a system variable. In this case we have used it to read the value of the *File$Type* variable associated with the filetype in question.

There is in fact a SWI call provided by RISC OS specifically to convert a filetype number to its corresponding string and vice versa (SWI **OS_FSControl** - see the PRM for details), which you should normally use if you need to perform this conversion yourself. However, we have used **OS_ReadVarVal** here in order to demonstrate that it is a useful SWI call for other similar purposes that may not have an alternative method provided.

ERROR-RETURNING SWI CALLS

You will have noticed that in line 3380 we have put an "X" before the name of the SWI. This requires a little explanation since this is a useful feature of SWI calls that we have not so far met in this book. Normally when a SWI call is made, the operating system or the module which handles the SWI will report any errors that occur directly to the user by means of a standard error box. However, if you precede the SWI name with an "X" as we have done here, the SWI returns *without* the error being reported, leaving it up to the calling task to decide what action to take (the task is notified that an error has occurred).

It is not always necessary to trap errors in this way, and you can usually use SWIs in their normal form as we have done so far throughout our listings, since if errors do occur you would normally want to know about them and it makes little difference whether they are reported by the operating system or the task. In this particular case, however, the most likely error generated by **OS_ReadVarVal** would occur if the system variable did not exist (as may well be the case for some filetypes). For the purposes of our program this is not really an error, but since we don't want to be bothered by an error box if this happens, we have used the X form of the SWI and simply ignored any error which results.

If we *had* wanted to deal with the error however, this would have been quite easy. If you use the X form of a SWI, an error is signalled by setting the overflow bit on return, and we can read the processor flags by adding a variable to the end of the SWI call after the last register to be returned, separated from the others by a semi-colon. The overflow bit is bit 0, so if we wanted to trap errors our call would look something like this:

```
    SYS "XOS_ReadVarVal","File$Type_"+type$,block%,255,
  0,3 TO ,,len%;flags%
    IF flags% AND 1 THEN PROCswi_error
    ...........
```

Note that if the call is not returning any registers, you must still include the TO before the semi-colon. For more information on error-returning SWI calls, see the PRM.

We have digressed a little here, so let's now return to the program. By the time we have executed line 3400, *obj$*, *type$* and *path$* have been set up to hold a description of the object type, its pathname and its filetype (including the textual description) respectively. **Wimp_GetWindowState** is called in lines 3410-3420 to ascertain if the window is already open. This is done by reading bit 16 of the window flags returned by the SWI call. If you look back at Figure 2.8 in Chapter 2, you will see that bits 16-20 of the window flags are used to return information about the window in question. For a full description you should read the section in the PRM covering **Wimp_CreateWindow**, but probably the most useful bit is the one we are using here (bit 16). If this is set, it means that the window is currently open. If our window *is* open, we force a redraw in line 3430 to ensure that the information displayed in the window is updated each time a new object is dragged to the application.

Once this is done, the new lines in *PROCredraw* (2845-2855) simply display in the window the three strings we have set up.

DATA TRANSFER PROTOCOL

So far we have looked at just one element of the data transfer protocol: the situation where a file is dragged from a directory display to our task. But a full implementation of the protocol requires up to four stages of communication between the tasks involved. First of all a task wishing to transfer data elsewhere must send a message to the intended recipient. The latter then acknowledges the first message with a second. The sender then transfers the data and sends a third message, which in turn is acknowledged by the recipient. Acorn has designed this protocol in such a way that it can be used for virtually all data transfer operations, whether from one application to another or from an application to the Filer when a file is to be saved.

The four messages concerned are action codes 1-4 in that order (see Figure 8.3). To re-cap, these are:

Message_DataSave
Message_DataSaveAck
Message_DataLoad
Message_DataLoadAck

We will cover the use of the full protocol by implementing a standard RISC OS save box in *OurTask*, but first we will describe the process of sending a message.

SENDING MESSAGES

We have already indicated that messages are sent by using the SWI **Wimp_SendMessage** (&400E7). The details of this call are shown in Figure 8.6.

On entry:

R0 = reason code (as returned by **Wimp_Poll**)
R1 = pointer to message block
R2 = task handle of destination task *or*
window handle (message sent to owner) *or*
-2 (message sent to owner of icon bar icon whose handle is in R3) *or*
0 (message broadcast to all tasks)
R3 = icon handle (if R2 = -2)

On exit:

R2 = task handle of destination task (except for broadcast messages)

Figure 8.6
Details of SWI "Wimp_SendMessage" (&400E7)

We have already looked at the basic format of the message block in Figure 8.1. When sending a message, you must fill in the length of the block at block+0, the action code at block+16, any data required from block+20 onwards (dependent on the action code), and if you are acknowledging a previous message, the sender's reference number at block+12. The Wimp itself will fill in the task handle of the sender (i.e. yours) at block+4, and will generate a unique reference number for the message at block+8. The block is updated before returning from the SWI so you can read this latter value at that point if you need it for future reference. As we have said, if you are acknowledging a previous message you must quote the reference number in your reply; all you need to do therefore when acknowledging is to copy the word at block+8 into block+12. This process is exactly like replying to a business letter; the sender quotes a *my_ref* reference, which you quote in turn as *your_ref*.

We have not said anything yet about the reason code in R0, other than that when receiving a message through **Wimp_Poll** the code is normally 17, 18 or 19. In fact, other poll reason codes can be used (for example you could send a task a message with a reason code of 2 to ask it to open a window), but normally you would have no reason to do so and we will not dwell on it here.

Reason codes 17 and 18 are similar to one another, being used to send a message to a destination task with an action code at block+16 as we have described. The difference between them is that reason code 18 expects the message to be acknowledged. In practice, provided that you follow the data transfer protocol correctly, you will know which messages to acknowledge from their action codes. Similarly, if our task has a need to respond to *Message_PreQuit* we know that we must acknowledge the message, and so for these cases we do not need separate procedures to handle the two reason codes. You may find, however, that if you are responding to some other message action codes you might need to differentiate between the two reason codes.

If your task sends a message with reason code 18, expecting an acknowledgment, and the recipient does not acknowledge, the Wimp will return the message to you with a reason code of 19. This is normally used to detect a situation where you are transferring data to another task but the task does not acknowledge that the data is received. You would then generate an error so that the user will know that the transfer has failed. We will be covering this when we describe the full data transfer protocol later in this chapter.

IMPLEMENTING A SAVE BOX

The multi-tasking nature of the Wimp means that there are a number of situations in which icons may be dragged from one task to another. The most common occurrence of this is associated with the standard save box used by many applications. To see one in operation, click Menu over the Palette icon on the icon bar, and then move the pointer across the arrow against the *Save* entry. This standard save box contains three icons: a sprite icon which is draggable, a writable text icon, and a menu icon with the legend *OK* (see Figure 8.7).

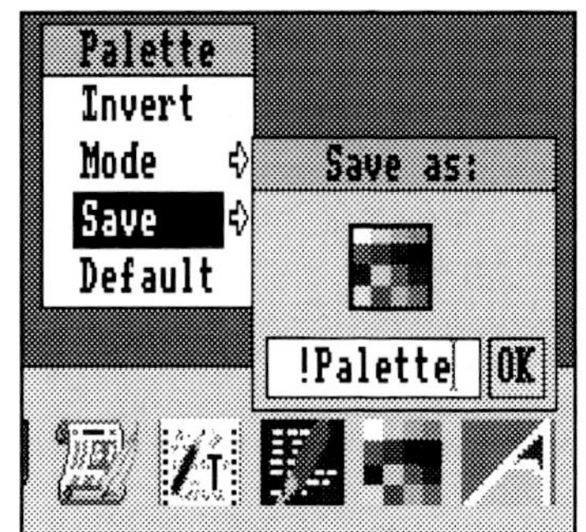

Figure 8.7
The Palette save box

To save a file (in this case a palette file), you can enter a filename (without a pathname) into the writable text icon and then drag the sprite icon to the directory display of your choice. From then on, whenever you open the save box from the menu, the last used pathname will be displayed in the writable icon (note that it is the job of the task to set the icon to contain the pathname - it is not done automatically by RISC OS). Files may now be saved by clicking on *OK* (or pressing Return) after optionally editing the filename supplied in the writable icon, or alternatively by just clicking on the *Save* entry in the menu.

To implement such a save box in our program, we have quite a bit of work to do. Firstly we must design the window for the save box with its three icons, and give the sprite icon a button type which will make it draggable. Then we must tie the save box in to a new entry on the icon bar menu. Next we must detect a drag via poll reason code 6 (mouse click), and respond using a SWI call to initiate the drag. Finally when the drag is completed (i.e. when the user releases the mouse button at the drag's destination), we must start the four-part message dialogue with the owner of the destination object (which will be the Filer if we are saving the file to a directory display). As if this were not enough, we must of course remember to save the data (using either SWI **OS_File** or Basic's file-handling commands).

Listing 8.4, when added to the existing *!RunImage* program, will implement a save box for *OurTask*. A *Save* option now appears on the icon bar menu, and moving the pointer over the arrow will display the familiar save box. Initially this will have the default filename "TestFile". You can then perform the save operation as described for palette files above. We don't actually have any sensible data to save from our program at this point, so all that is saved is a text file containing the three strings *obj$*, *path$* and *type$* - in other words the details of the last object dragged to the application.

Because Listing 8.4 is quite complex you should be very careful when typing it in.

Listing 8.4

```
 230 DIM sbspr% 8,sbtext% 255,sbval% 3
 240 $sbspr%="file_fff":$sbtext%="TestFile"
 250 $sbval%="A~ "
 370 save%=FNcreate_window(0,0,264,164,0,0,&84000012,"Save as:")
 380 a%=FNcreate_icon(save%,100,-92,68,68,&6102,"",sbspr%,1,9)
 390 a%=FNcreate_icon(save%,8,-156,192,48,&700F12D,"",sbtext%,sbval%,256)
 400 a%=FNcreate_icon(save%,208,-156,48,48,&C701903D,"OK",0,0,0)
 610 WHEN 7:PROCstartsave
 660 WHEN 19:PROCreport("Transfer failed - receiver died",1)
1230 block%?38=2
1530 WHEN save%:CASE block%!16 OF
1540 WHEN 0:IF block%!8 AND 64 PROCdragbox
1550 WHEN 2:IF block%!8 AND 5 PROCquicksave
1560 ENDCASE
1570 ENDCASE
1720 WHEN key%=13 AND !block%=save%
1730 PROCquicksave
1735
2260 WHEN 2:PROCshowmenu(imenu%,!block%-64,228)
2610 WHEN 1:PROCquicksave
2620 WHEN 2:quit%=TRUE
3230 WHEN 2:PROCdatasave
4000 DEF PROCstartsave
4010 SYS "Wimp_GetPointerInfo",,block%
4020 block%!20=block%!12:block%!24=block%!16
4030 block%!28=!block%:block%!32=block%!4
4040 block%!36=LENobj$+LENpath$+LENtype$+23
4050 !block%=64:block%!12=0
```

```
 4060 block%!16=1:block%!40=&FFF
 4070 $(block%+44)=FNgetleaf($sbtext%)
 4080 SYS "Wimp_SendMessage",18,block%,block%!20,bloc
k%!24
 4090 ENDPROC
 4100 :
 4200 DEF PROCquicksave
 4210 IF INSTR($sbtext%,".") THEN
 4220 PROCsaveit
 4230 ELSE
 4240 PROCreport("To save, drag the icon to a directo
ry viewer",1)
 4250 ENDIF
 4260 ENDPROC
 4270 :
 4300 DEF PROCsaveit
 4310 file%=OPENOUT($sbtext%)
 4320 BPUT#file%,obj$
 4330 BPUT#file%,"Filename: "+path$
 4340 BPUT#file%,"Filetype: "+type$
 4350 CLOSE#file%
 4360 OSCLI "SetType "+$sbtext%+" FFF"
 4370 ENDPROC
 4380 :
 4400 DEF FNgetleaf(a$)
 4410 WHILE INSTR(a$,".")
 4420 a$=MID$(a$,INSTR(a$,".")+1)
 4430 ENDWHILE
 4440 =a$+CHR$0
 4450 :
 4500 DEF PROCdatasave
 4510 $sbtext%=FNstring(block%+44)
 4520 PROCsaveit
 4530 block%!12=block%!8
 4540 block%!16=3:!block%=256
 4550 SYS "Wimp_SendMessage",18,block%,block%!20,bloc
k%!24
 4560 ENDPROC
 4570 :
 4600 DEF PROCdragbox
 4610 !block%=save%
 4620 SYS "Wimp_GetWindowState",,block%
```

```
 4630 ox%=block%!4-block%!20
 4640 oy%=block%!16-block%!24
 4650 block%!4=0
 4660 SYS "Wimp_GetIconState",,block%
 4670 block%!4=5:block%!8=ox%+block%!8
 4680 block%!12=oy%+block%!12
 4690 block%!16=ox%+block%!16
 4700 block%!20=oy%+block%!20
 4710 block%!24=0:block%!28=0
 4720 block%!32=&7FFFFFFF
 4730 block%!36=&7FFFFFFF
 4740 SYS "Wimp_DragBox",,block%
 4750 ENDPROC
 4760 :
20000 DATA OurTask,3,0,info%,Info,0,save%,Save,&80,-1
,Quit
```

As you can imagine, there is quite a bit of explaining to do here, but the actual process is quite straightforward so if you study it carefully you should be able to see what is going on. Incidentally, can you see why we have included line 1230? We will explain this at the end of the chapter.

First of all we have created the save box itself at line 370, together with its icons at lines 380-400. The sprite icon and writable icon are both indirected, so we have reserved blocks of memory for the sprite name and for the writable icon's text. The latter is given the default value of "TestFile". We have also set up a validation string for the writable icon ("A~ ") because the space character is not allowed in filenames (refer back to Chapter 5 if you are unclear about the meaning of this validation string). All this is done at lines 230-250. Note that we have allowed a buffer length of 256 for the writable icon because pathnames can be quite lengthy. Acorn recommends that tasks should be able to handle names of at least 256 characters.

The name of the sprite we have used is *file_fff*. We mentioned in Chapter 5 that a number of sprites were already available in the Wimp sprite pool, and this is one of them, being the icon which is used for text files (type &FFF). In order to access this, we have used an indirected icon with the middle word of the 12 bytes of icon data set to 1 for the Wimp sprite pool (see Figure 5.6). The way in which we assert that a particular icon is draggable is by specifying an appropriate button type in the icon's flags. We have used a button type of 6 for our draggable sprite icon (see Figure 5.5). This behaves as follows: a click notifies the task, while a drag returns a button state shifted left by 4 bits. Thus if **Wimp_Poll** returns a reason code of 6 (mouse click) with a button pressed value of 1 or 4 it means that the icon has been clicked with Adjust or Select respectively, but if 16 or 64 is returned, it means that a drag has been initiated (defined as a button press with Select or Adjust of more than about one fifth of a second).

Having amended the menu data at line 20000 and also the menu selection routine at lines 2610-2620, in order to add the *Save* option to the menu, we now need to detect when a drag has been made from the save box. We can do this by making some amendments to *PROCclick* in lines 1530-1550. We have added a line to our CASE statement to detect clicks over the save box (line 1530), and this leads to a second CASE statement which examines the icon. If this is icon 0 (the sprite icon) and the button state is 64 (i.e. a drag with Select) then *PROCdragbox* is called (line 1540). If the icon is 2 (the *OK* icon) and either Select or Adjust has been clicked (line 1550), *PROCquicksave* is called. We will come back to this shortly.

OBJECT DRAGGING

Staying with our drag, *PROCdragbox* performs the process of actually putting a drag box on the screen, which can then be moved around with the pointer in the usual way. When the drag is finished (i.e. the user releases the mouse button), the Wimp notifies the task using poll reason code 7, which we will consider in a moment.

The drag is initiated by calling SWI **Wimp_DragBox** (&400D0). The parameter block required by this call is given in Figure 8.8. Since the co-ordinates must be given as screen co-ordinates relative to the graphics origin, we must call **Wimp_GetWindowState** to discover the position of the origin of the work area of the parent window relative to the screen origin (lines 4610-4640) before we can make the call to **Wimp_DragBox**. We also make a call to **Wimp_GetIconState** (lines 4650-4660) to find the co-ordinates of the icon to be dragged relative to the work area origin (otherwise we would not know where to start with the drag box). The data supplied at block+24 to block+36 represent the co-ordinates of the boundary of the drag, i.e. the total area within which the icon can be dragged around. This is made as large as possible (lines 4710-4730) since we do not want to restrict our drag to a particular area. The *drag type* at block+4 determines the visual appearance of the drag box. The PRM supplies details of eleven different types of drag operation, some of which include rubber banding facilities, but for most purposes drag type 5 will suffice: *drag fixed size "rotating dash" box*. This gives the familiar box that you see whenever you move an icon around.

R1 = pointer to block
or if set to <=0 means cancel drag

block+4	drag type
8	minimum x co-ordinate of drag box at start
12	minimum y co-ordinate of drag box at start
16	maximum x co-ordinate of drag box at start
20	maximum y co-ordinate of drag box at start
24	minimum x co-ordinate of bounding box
28	minimum y co-ordinate of bounding box
32	maximum x co-ordinate of bounding box
36	maximum y co-ordinate of bounding box

Figure 8.8
Parameter block for SWI "Wimp_DragBox"
as applicable to drag type 5

We now have a drag box which will follow the pointer around the screen as the mouse is moved. At some point the user will release the mouse button, indicating that this is the intended destination of the drag. When this happens, the Wimp returns a poll reason code of 7 (user drag box) to our task, which is picked up at line 610 and activates a call to *PROCstartsave*. The block returned with this reason code contains the co-ordinates of the drag box, but these are of little use to us on their own since we need to know the window handle so that we can strike up a dialogue with the owner.

PROCstartsave therefore calls **Wimp_GetPointerInfo** (at line 4010) to find out the pointer position at the end of the drag, together with the window (and possibly icon) handle. Details of this SWI were given in Figure 6.2 in Chapter 6. The function of the rest of the procedure is to set up the parameter block for *Message_DataSave*, which forms the first leg of the data transfer protocol. The message block required for this action code is shown in Figure 8.9.

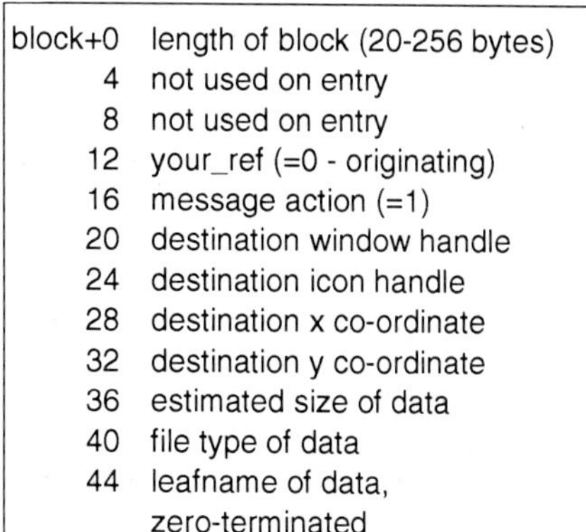

block+0	length of block (20-256 bytes)
4	not used on entry
8	not used on entry
12	your_ref (=0 - originating)
16	message action (=1)
20	destination window handle
24	destination icon handle
28	destination x co-ordinate
32	destination y co-ordinate
36	estimated size of data
40	file type of data
44	leafname of data, zero-terminated

Figure 8.9
Message block for **Message_DataSave**

As you can see, the window and icon handles together with the co-ordinates of the destination are extracted from the block returned by **Wimp_GetPointerInfo** and placed in the correct position for *Message_DataSave* (lines 4020-4030). Since we are using the same block of memory for both calls, we need to be a little careful about the order in which we take data from the first call and move it around in preparation for making the second. For the estimated size of the file at block+36 (line 4040) we have simply added together the lengths of the strings which will form the file, and added 23 bytes to cover linefeeds and also the addition of the words "Filename:" and "Filetype:" which will be added to *path$* and *type$* respectively when the file is saved. By referring to Figures 8.9 and 8.6 you should be able to work out what the remainder of *PROCstartsave* is doing, culminating with the actual sending of the message at line 4080.

Provided that the drag has ended at an object owned by a task which can respond to a drag (e.g. the Filer), the next stage is that our task will receive a *Message_DataAck* (action code 2) containing the full pathname for the save (at block+44). We pick this up by including the appropriate line in *PROCreceive* (line 3230), which responds to action code 2 by calling *PROCdatasave*. This procedure places the full pathname of the object into the save box writable icon (line 4510), calls *PROCsaveit* to save the data, and sends *Message_DataLoad* back to the destination task. All we need to do here is to copy *my_ref* from the previous message into *your_ref* (line 4530), change the action code to 3 and the block size to 256 to cater for the maximum length of name (line 4540), and make the call to **Wimp_SendMessage** (line 4550). Finally the receiver sends us a *Message_DataLoadAck* to indicate that the protocol has been successfully completed.

All we need to do now is to detect whether acknowledgments are received when we expect them, and this is where our poll reason code 19 comes in. If a task does not acknowledge a message of ours when it should do so (i.e. a message sent with reason code 18), the Wimp will return a reason code of 19 to us. Since our task only ever sends messages when it wants to save data, we know that if we receive reason code 19 it means that something has gone wrong with the data transfer. Line 660 in the poll loop is therefore all we need in order to generate an error if this reason code is ever received.

We have now completed the description of the dialogue between our task and the recipient of the data we wish to save. This will seem complex at first, but do please study it carefully and re-read any sections which are unclear at first. Like all other aspects of the Wimp, there is a lot of detail to be mastered but once this is done it is really quite logical and straightforward to implement.

SAVING DATA

At some point along the line, we do of course have to save our data. We have done this immediately after receiving *Message_DataSaveAck*, by calling *PROCsaveit* in line 4520. This procedure simply creates a file using the pathname supplied with *Message_DataSaveAck*, and outputs the strings as we have mentioned earlier, using Basic's own file-handling statements. If we had just wanted to save a block of memory (as we might if our task was a text editor, for example), we could have used SWI **OS_File** instead (see the PRM for details).

There is one loose end still to be picked up. We said earlier that a click on the *OK* icon in the save box would activate *PROCquicksave*. This provides a shortcut to saving the data without requiring a drag, but in accordance with the standard procedure laid down by Acorn, this should only work if there is a full pathname in the writable icon, just as we saw earlier with the Palette save box. *PROCquicksave* therefore scans the filename for a full stop character. If it finds one, it assumes that the name includes a full pathname and calls *PROCsaveit* without any further ado. Note that there is no need at all for the message dialogue in this case since our task knows exactly where to save the file and can just use normal filing procedures without any discussion with the Filer.

If there is no full stop in the string, an error is generated with the message "To save, drag the icon to a directory viewer". You will probably be familiar with this message from other applications, and in fact this is the standard practice recommended by Acorn for such situations.

PROCquicksave is also called if the user clicks on the *Save* option on the menu (line 2610) rather than opening the save box. And finally, it is usual for pressing Return inside the save box's writable icon to have the same effect as clicking on *OK*. We have therefore amended *PROCkeypress* so that *PROCquicksave* is called if a key code of 13 is detected within the save box (lines 1720-1730).

SUBMENU WARNINGS

We have almost finished our look at the Wimp's message system, but there is one more useful action code to consider - *Message_MenuWarning* (action code &400C0). We mentioned earlier that this is generated if the user moves the pointer over a submenu arrow, provided that the message bit (bit 3) of the menu flags has been set for the parent item (see the description of **Wimp_CreateMenu** in Chapter 6). If the task does not respond to this message, then the submenu will not appear. The point of the message is to allow the task to modify or process any data *before* opening the submenu. For example, a dialogue box might display the results of calculations which need to be updated at the time the box is displayed, or a save box might wish to use an icon for one of several different filetypes depending on the circumstances under which the box is opened. The message block returned by *Message_MenuWarning* is shown in Figure 8.10.

block+20	submenu pointer from menu item
24	x co-ordinate of top left of new submenu
28	y co-ordinate of top left of new submenu
32	item selected from main menu
36	item selected from first submenu
....	
block+n	-1 to terminate list

Figure 8.10
Message block returned by
Message_MenuWarning

The pointer at block+20 is the original submenu pointer (or window handle) contained in the menu definition that would have been used if the menu flag had not been set. The task may use this same pointer to open the submenu, or it may substitute it with another. The words at block+32 onwards tell the task which menu item is currently being accessed, and are interpreted in exactly the same way as the menu selection block returned with poll reason code 9, and described in Chapter 6. It can be useful to have this information if there is more than one item which may generate a *Message_MenuWarning*.

Once you have carried out any actions you need to do before opening the submenu, you just call SWI **Wimp_CreateSubMenu** (&400E8). Details of this call are given in Figure 8.11, and all you need to do is to take the parameters from block+20 - block+28 (altering the submenu pointer if you need to), and place them into R1-R3.

R1 = pointer to submenu block
R2 = x co-ordinate of top left of submenu
R3 = y co-ordinate of top left of submenu

Figure 8.11
Parameters for SWI "Wimp_CreateSubMenu" (&400E8)

To demonstrate how this works in practice, we will add a routine to *OurTask* which alters the filetype icon in the save box in a random fashion each time the box is opened. Add Listing 8.5 to *!RunImage* and run the program. Now when you move the pointer across the submenu arrow on the *Save* option, the icon will show any one of four filetypes, and these will appear at random.

Listing 8.5

```
  3250 WHEN &400C0:PROCsubmenu
  4800 DEF PROCsubmenu
  4810 CASE RND(4) OF
  4820 WHEN 1:$sbspr%="file_fff"
  4830 WHEN 2:$sbspr%="file_ffb"
  4840 WHEN 3:$sbspr%="file_ffd"
  4850 WHEN 4:$sbspr%="file_ff9"
  4860 ENDCASE
  4870 SYS "Wimp_CreateSubMenu",,block%!20,block%!24,b
lock%!28
  4880 ENDPROC
  4890 :
 20000 DATA OurTask,3,0,info%,Info,8,save%,Save,&80,-1
,Quit
```

The listing should be quite easy to understand. First of all our menu definition must be altered so that bit 3 is set for the *Save* option (by putting a value of 8 for the menu flags in line 20000). Next a line must be added to *PROCreceive* to detect the *Message_MenuWarning* (line 3250). This calls *PROCsubmenu*, which merely sets the sprite name for the sprite icon to one of four values depending on a random number (lines 4810-4860). These are all sprites from the Wimp sprite pool, and should be familiar to you as they are all common filetypes. Finally **Wimp_CreateSubMenu** is called with the values which were returned in the message block.

INPUT FOCUS

In our description of Listing 8.4 we asked why we had changed line 1230 in *FNcreate_window*. If you refer back to Figure 2.3 you will see that the value at block+38 sets the title bar background colour when the window has the input focus. If you adhere to Acorn's guidelines, this will normally be cream (colour 12). However, the guidelines also state that dialogue boxes should *not* be highlighted but should remain grey (colour 2). Our save box falls into this category, and therefore we have altered *FNcreate_window* since none of our other windows require the input focus. Normally, however, you would need to add an additional parameter to the function so that you can differentiate between windows which require to be highlighted and those which do not.

Once again, this has been a complex chapter with a great deal of detail to be grasped. If you have managed to stay with us so far you should by now have a good understanding of the Wimp and are probably capable of writing your own multi-tasking programs. If you are still floundering, don't lose heart - go back to the point at which you started to become lost and study the text and the listings carefully. There *is* light at the end of the tunnel, and the best way to get there is to look carefully at each procedure in the listings, and wherever possible experiment with them - "hands on" experience is far more valuable in understanding Wimp programming than endlessly ploughing your way through pages of theory. This is not to say that the theory is unimportant, but you are more likely to see the logic behind it if you try to relate it to practical ideas.

If light relief is possible with such a weighty subject as the Wimp, the next chapter will provide it, as we shall be abandoning theory and describing a tool which will make the job of designing windows very much easier.

9. Templates

What is a template? - Using FormEd - Creating a window - Adding some icons - Sprite-only icons - Text-plus-sprite icons - Using templates in an application - Using sprites from more than one area

WHAT IS A TEMPLATE?

So far in our test application we have defined all our windows within the program itself, by making use of the function *FNcreate_window* which was described in Chapter 2. However, there is a more effective way of creating windows, and that is to use *templates.* A template is a complete window definition (including icons) which can be stored in a file and loaded into a program when required. Three Wimp SWI calls have been provided to enable you to use template files, and what is more, Acorn has provided an application, *FormEd,* to assist you in designing your windows. This takes all the guesswork out of the job and will also create your template file for you when the design is completed. With FormEd, you design all your windows on screen, and you can see exactly how they look, complete with all their icons, while you edit the design at will until it meets your requirements. Most commercial applications use this method, and if you look inside almost any application directory (e.g. that for Maestro) you will find a file called *Templates* (Figure 9.1). This file will contain one or more templates which define the windows used by the application.

FormEd is widely available, and can be supplied by most Acorn dealers for a modest sum. It is also included on the RISC User *Wimp Programmer's Toolkit* (details of which are given in Appendix F).

Because templates are used to create windows and icons, you will probably find it helpful to refer back regularly to Chapters 2 and 5, where these elements of the Wimp were fully described.

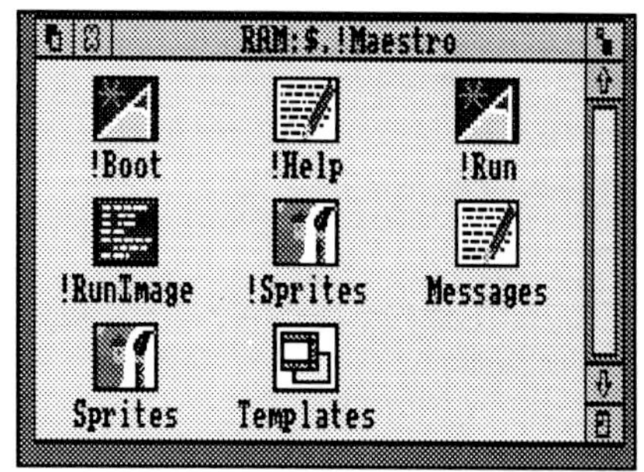

Figure 9.1
Maestro's application directory showing the Templates *file*

USING FormEd

FormEd is supplied with a Help file which constitutes a very brief manual for the product, and it may be worth taking a look at this file before using the program.

You start FormEd just like any other application, by double-clicking on its icon in a directory viewer, or by double-clicking on a template file (but note that if you double-click on a template file once FormEd is installed, a *second* copy of the application will be installed to handle the second file). Before you start to create any windows of your own, it is well worth having a look at some templates from other applications, for example Edit. In RISC OS 2, open up the application directory and double-click on the *Templates* file. In RISC OS 3, choose *Open '$'* from the Resources icon bar menu, double-click on the *Resources* directory, then the *Edit* directory, and finally on the file *Templates*. What happens now will depend on which version of FormEd you have. Earlier versions (prior to 1.24) display all the windows defined in the file on the screen at the same time (see Figure 9.2), while versions 1.24 onwards show a list of templates in a window (Figure 9.3), each of which can then be displayed by double-clicking. You could try editing some of Edit's windows by way of experiment, but be careful not to save back the results and thus overwrite the original.

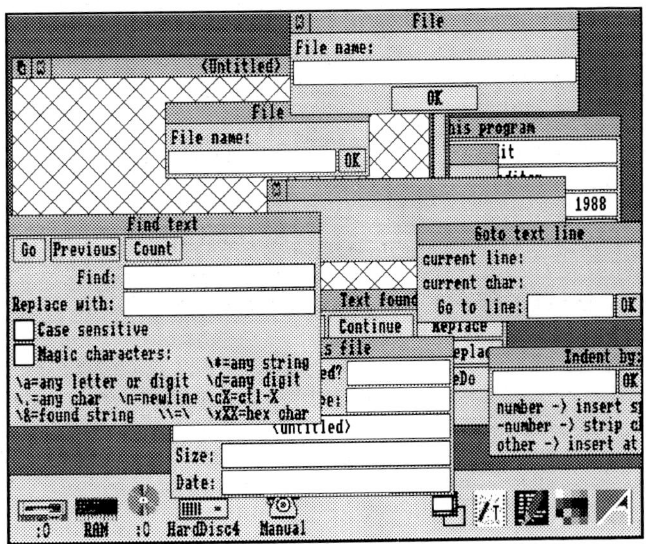

Figure 9.2
Edit's templates displayed on the screen

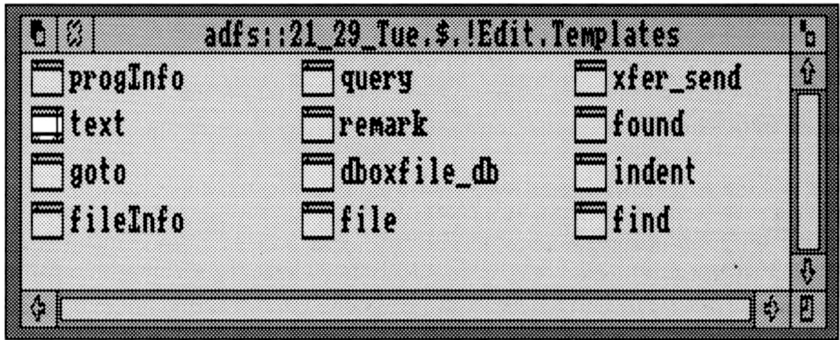

Figure 9.3
The later version of FormEd opens a window listing the templates

CREATING A WINDOW

To illustrate the use of FormEd, we will go back to the *OurTask* program in the state it was in after adding Listing 7.1 in Chapter 7. If you remember, the program at that point displayed a set of radio icons from which to choose a temperature scale, and a coloured bar showing values for boiling point, freezing point and absolute zero for the selected scale (see Figure 7.3). Using FormEd, we will design the main window on screen and load it in as a template file instead of creating it as part of the program listing. To avoid confusion between this program and *OurTask* in its later updated form, make a copy of the *!OurTask* application as it stood at Listing 7.1, and call this copy *!PlateTest*. This is the application that we will now be working on in this chapter.

First of all, install FormEd on the icon bar and click on its icon. If you are using the earlier version of FormEd, this action itself will create a new window, and will display it on the screen ready for editing.

The later version opens a window of its own within which it will display a list of all the windows you create; to create a new one just click Menu over the FormEd window and move across *New window*. A writable icon will appear into which you should type the identifier. This is the name you choose for the window (maximum 11 characters), and will be used to identify that particular window in the template file when your application needs to load it. For our application, we will use the name *Main*. Once this is done, an icon bearing the identifier will appear in the FormEd window, and this can be opened for editing by double-clicking on it.

Drag out the new window to the approximate size that it will be when the design is finished. Note that this is the initial visible area that you are determining - the work area extent will be set later. It is a good idea to allow a little extra for the visible area at this stage - you can always alter the window again later to make it just the size you want. Now click Menu over the window. The menu which appears is divided into two parts, the upper part dealing with icons - most of which is initially greyed out (since we have not yet created any icons) - and the lower part with the window itself. Move the pointer across the *Window flags* entry, and if the *New format* option is not already ticked, click on it to tick it. If you refer back to Figure 2.8 in Chapter 2, you will see that certain window flags were marked as "Unused" because they only applied to an earlier version of the window manager. The *New format* option simply ensures that these bits are not used by mistake when creating a RISC OS application.

Now take a look at the various options below the dotted line in the *Window flags* submenu. These all relate to parts of the window (scroll bars, Close icon etc.), and initially all will be ticked, but you can unset any of these by choosing the corresponding menu option. The results will be shown immediately in the window. Thus if you untick *H scroll* your window will lose its horizontal scroll bar, and so on. Our window does not need scroll bars or an Adjust size icon, so these can be unticked, but it is better to do this later, since if you remove the scroll bars too early you would need to replace them again if you want to alter the window size within FormEd while you are editing your design.

Next move the pointer across the *Title icon* entry in the Window flags submenu to display the *Title flags* submenu for the window. Then move across the *Text* entry, and type in the required text for the title bar. If you type in more than 12 characters, FormEd will automatically make it indirected, ticking the *Indirected* entry on the submenu and setting the length of the buffer accordingly (actually to 1 character more than the current length of the title text, to allow for a terminator at the end of the string). You can alter the length of the buffer yourself if you need to by moving across the *Indirected* entry and typing a value into the writable icon. You may need to do this if, for example, you expect the contents of the window title to change while the program is running; you would then make the length of the buffer equal to the maximum expected length of the title.

To make things relatively simple we will not use an indirected title string, so you should type *Temperature* into the writable icon. This will now be displayed in the window title bar.

Turning our attention to entries above the dotted line on the *Window flags* submenu, we can alter the flags which determine a number of further options. If you refer back to Chapter 2 again, you will see that each of these items on the submenu relates to one of the window flags. For example, the *Moveable* option determines whether bit 1 (window can be dragged) is set, while *No bounds* relates to bit 6 (window can extend outside screen area). Bit 4 (Wimp needs no help to redraw) is handled by the *Auto-redraw* option; if you untick this item, the window will become cross-hatched. This is merely a reminder that you have turned off the auto-redraw flag for this window, and that you will therefore need a redraw routine in the Wimp application which will use the template. The cross-hatching will not appear when the window is opened in your program. In listing 7.1, we created our window with this bit unset since we wished to redraw parts of the window ourselves, but this time we are going to do it all using icons, so you can leave this option ticked. You should also ensure the *Moveable* option is ticked; all the others can remain unset.

If you were to untick the *Moveable* option it would mean of course that your window would not be movable when it manifests itself in your application. But it also makes it unmovable from within FormEd. This is because FormEd treats the windows and icons which you are creating in just the same way as any other Wimp task. The window you are editing will even respond to a click on the Close icon - but if you are using the earlier version of FormEd, beware, as this will delete it completely. The fact that FormEd treats all windows and icons you are editing as normal windows and icons can initially be a source of confusion, but it soon becomes clear as you use the application.

You will notice that the *Window flags* submenu has a *Work area* entry, in addition to the *Work area* item on the main *Window* menu. In fact the item on the submenu is to allow you to set the button type for the window's work area (bits 12-15 of the work area flags - see Figure 2.10). If you move across the entry to the *Button type* submenu, you will see that the items on that submenu correspond to the button types shown in Figure 2.10. For the purpose of our window, we can leave *Click* ticked.

Going back to the top level *Window* menu, the *Colours* entry, as you might expect, allows you to set the colours for the various parts of the window, as described in detail in Chapter 2. If you have not already experimented with window colours when running the program listings in that chapter, you will find it easy to play around with the colours in FormEd using this submenu. However, as we have stressed before, you should always follow Acorn's guidelines with regard to window colours. FormEd's default colours are set up to conform to this standard, and you should not change them when writing your own applications unless you have a very good reason to do so. Thus you will find that the title bar and work area foreground colours will be colour 7 (black), the title bar background colour 2, the work area background and the scroll bar inner area colour 1, and the scroll bar outer area colour 3. The entry entitled *Input focus* determines the title bar background colour when the window has the input focus, i.e. when the caret is in the window.

Moving across the *Work area* entry on the top level menu enables you to alter the work area extent of the window. This brings up a dialogue box which contains a number of arrow icons which may be clicked on to alter the work area extent. In all cases, you cannot make this less than the visible work area currently displayed by the window. Once you have set up suitable values, click on *OK*. The work area extent really only needs to be set if you are creating a window whose visible area may not always cover the whole window, and which therefore has scroll bars. Many simple applications will display all their information in one fixed-size window without scroll bars, and in these cases the setting of the work area extent is irrelevant. The window we are creating for *PlateTest* falls into this category, and so you do not need to worry about the settings in the *Work area extent* dialogue box.

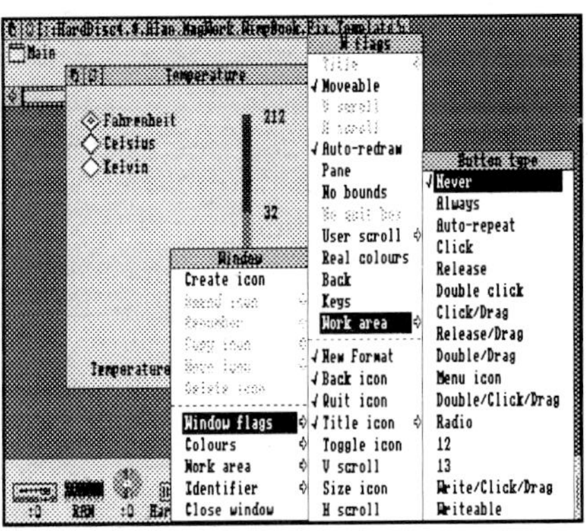

Using FormEd to design a window template

Finally, if you are using the early version of FormEd you need to give your window an identifier, since this will not have been done otherwise. Move the pointer across the *Identifier* entry in the top level menu, type in a suitable name (*Main* in our example), and note it down (since you will need to specify the name when you load the template from your program). If you are creating more than one window, you need to take special care to give them all an identifier, because FormEd will only remind you if *none* of your windows has one, and when you come to save your templates it will only save those with identifiers. This will only be a problem with the earlier FormEd, since with the later version you cannot create a window without specifying an identifier first.

ADDING SOME ICONS

Creating icons in FormEd is easy. Just choose the *Create icon* option from the *Window* menu, and an icon will be put into the window. Initially it will be a simple text icon in black on cream, bearing the legend *<Untitled>*, but with FormEd it is easy to alter any or all of the parameters which determine the icon's appearance. You will find that the icon is draggable. If you use the Select button you can drag the icon to anywhere within the parent window to reposition it. If you use Adjust on the other hand you will be able to drag its edges so as to resize it.

For our first icon we will create a simple text icon - the one at the bottom of the window which reads "Temperature scale". First of all drag the icon down towards the bottom of the visible area of the window. Now click Menu over the icon, and move the pointer across the *Amend icon* entry. This brings up a menu of icon flags, and these can be selected or deselected as required, in just the same way as the window flags. If you refer back to Figure 5.4, you will see that once again the menu entries correspond to the flags, apart from bits 21-23 which FormEd does not cater for (these bits would normally be set or unset by the application according to circumstances, and so it is not necessary to define them at the outset).

Since this will be a text icon, ensure that *Text* is ticked and that *Sprite* is unticked. Now move across the *Text* entry, type in *Temperature scale* and press Return. This is more than 12 characters in length, and so FormEd will automatically make it indirected in just the same way as for the window title text. It will also enlarge the icon if the text will not fit the original size.

You can now alter the other flags as required. In this case, we do not want a border, nor do we want the icon filled, so we will untick both the *Border* and *Filled* items. We will also want to alter the button type of the icon. By default this will be *Click/drag* (button type 6). We do not want to respond to clicks or drags on this particular icon, so we will need to choose the *Never* option (button type 0), but if you make this selection you will not be able to move or resize the icon from within FormEd. It is usually best to leave the button type as *Click/drag* until you have finished editing, and then alter it to your chosen type.

One important point to note down on paper about your icon is its number. This is supplied in the second entry of the top level menu. It will read *Amend icon #0* for the first icon, *Amend icon #1* for the second, and so on. You need to know this number, because this is the icon handle by which you will identify that icon in any dialogue with the Wimp. You can renumber any icon at any time using the *Renumber* option from the menu and entering the new number in the writable icon provided. If you supply a new number that already belongs to an existing icon, FormEd will swap the numbers of the two icons - very handy providing you know what is going on.

The *Copy icon, Move icon* and *Delete icon* entries on the top level menu need little explanation, except to add that *Move icon* moves the icon by a pixel at a time in the required direction. This is handy for making small adjustments to an icon's position, especially if you have already altered the button type to something other than *Click/drag*. The later version of FormEd also allows you to position an icon at specific co-ordinates within a window.

SPRITE-ONLY ICONS

In order to illustrate the creation of a sprite-only icon, we will use this method for our coloured bar on the right of the window. First of all you must create a sprite. Load up Paint, open a sprite file window, and create a mode 12 sprite called *Bar,* 100 pixels high by 10 pixels wide. Now fill the top half of this rectangle with red and the bottom half with blue. Save the sprite file inside the *!PlateTest* directory as *Sprites.*

Now return to FormEd and create a new icon. Make sure that the *Text* option is unticked, but for the moment leave the *Indirected* option unticked. Then tick *Sprite,* and move the pointer across this option to type in the sprite name *Bar.* Sprites in the Wimp pool are loaded into FormEd automatically at start-up from a sprite file called *Default* within FormEd's application directory; if our icon were to contain one of these, the sprite would automatically appear in the icon. However, we are using our own sprite so we must notify FormEd about it. We can do this by dragging the sprite file to FormEd. If it is dragged to the icon bar icon, any sprites in the file will now replace the default set. If on the other hand it is dragged into the window you are editing, the sprite file will be merged with the default set.

If you are using both Wimp pool sprites and user sprites in the same program, you will therefore need to drag your sprite file to the window to merge the sprites, since otherwise you will only see one set displayed on the screen. *PlateTest* will be using sprites from both areas, so you must follow this procedure if you want all the sprites to be visible in FormEd.

Assuming that the sprite is now displayed correctly, you will find that you need to re-size the icon so that it is the same size and shape as the sprite. Having done this you can then position it at the correct place in the window, remove the border, and set the button type to *Never.*

TEXT-PLUS-SPRITE ICONS

When we described icons in Chapter 5, we considered text-plus-sprite icons, and we created a set of radio icons of this type. It is quite easy to do this in FormEd, and we will demonstrate by creating the same three icons for use in *PlateTest*. To avoid a lot of unnecessary editing, it is easiest to create one icon first, set all the parameters and then copy it twice, altering the text of the other two icons afterwards.

First of all, then, we must create an icon, then tick both the *Text* and *Sprite* entries. The text should be typed into the writable icon relating to the *Text* entry as before (in our case the first icon is labelled *Fahrenheit*, so this is what we should type in). As we saw in Chapter 5, the icon must be indirected and the sprite name must be included in a validation string, preceded by an S command. In fact, it *is* possible to have non-indirected text-plus-sprite icons, but they are of little practical value since both the text and the sprite name must be the same (because there is only one 12-character block for this purpose in the icon definition). So wherever you use text-plus-sprite icons you would normally make them indirected.

As far as FormEd is concerned, then, you should leave the writable icon which forms the *Sprite name* submenu blank, move the pointer across the *Indirected* entry and then across *Valid*, and type in *Sradiooff,radioon*. If you are unclear about the meaning of this validation string, refer back to the description of Listing 5.5 in Chapter 5.

Provided that you have dragged your sprite file into the window in order to ensure that the default set of sprites is not overwritten, you should now see the *radiooff* sprite displayed in your icon, but it will most likely appear in the centre of the icon, overwritten by the text. However, as we described in Chapter 5, it is possible to specify the relative positions of the two elements in a text-plus-sprite icon, using a combination of the horizontal, vertical and right-justified bits. In the case of radio icons, you should tick the *V centred* option and untick both the *H centred* and *R justified* options. This will position the sprite to the left, with the text just to the right of it.

The text and sprite should now be displayed in the correct places, but there is still a little work to be done. For a start, the text will probably overrun the icon border at the right-hand side, so you will need to drag out the icon's size with Adjust to contain it. Now you must remove the border, set the background colour to the same as the window background colour (normally 1), set the button type to *Radio*, and finally give the icon a non-zero ESG number. Having done all this, you can now copy the icon twice. The new icons will still be labelled *Fahrenheit* but you can alter the text to

Celsius and *Kelvin* in turn. All the icons are as yet unselected, but clicking on any one of them will select that icon and switch its sprite to *radioon*. Provided that the ESG numbers are the same for the whole group, the icons will now behave in the correct way: clicking on any of them will select it and deselect the others. You should note when using FormEd that whichever icon is selected in the window at the time the template file is saved, will also be selected when the template is loaded and the window created in your program.

Two things now remain to be done before we can use the template in our program. Firstly we must create icons which will display the figures for boiling point, freezing point and absolute zero. These will be text-only icons, indirected so that we can update them whenever the temperature scale is changed. You should find it quite simple to create these in FormEd - the *Text*, *V centred* and *Indirected* options should be ticked, and the button type should be *Never*. Assuming that you have selected the *Fahrenheit* icon in the radio group, the initial values to be typed into the *Text* writable icons will be *212*, *32* and *-523* respectively.

Finally, we must return to our sprite-only icon (the coloured bar). You will remember that we left the *Indirected* option unticked, but in fact the icon must be indirected, otherwise we cannot display the sprite in our program (since only an indirected sprite icon has provision for a sprite area pointer). The reason we left it unticked is that FormEd cannot display sprites in indirected sprite-only icons. This is merely a limitation of the way in which FormEd works, and does not affect our own program in any way. You must therefore now set the indirected bit for this icon. The sprite will disappear from the window you are editing, but provided that you have correctly sized the icon, this will not matter at this stage.

And that's all there is to it. Now you can move the window to the position on screen where you wish it to appear when it is first opened in your program, adjust the size as required, and remove the scroll bars and the Toggle size icon. Now save the template. With the earlier version of FormEd, you choose the *Save templates* option from the icon bar menu, and drag the template icon to an application directory, using the default name *Templates*. The later version has a similar option on the main window menu. This will save all the windows present in the editor (in the case of *PlateTest* just the one), together with all their icons. The *Quit* option can now be used to exit FormEd - but note that with the earlier version this option kills its task without any warning, even if you haven't saved the last two hours' work!

This may all sound a very long-winded way of designing windows and icons, but in fact it is much quicker and easier than doing it by trial and error. Once you have used FormEd a couple of times you will marvel at the way you can fine-tune your design knowing that every alteration you make will be reflected immediately on the screen as you edit.

USING TEMPLATES IN AN APPLICATION

Having created a window template for use by *PlateTest,* we can now introduce the program listing. As we said earlier, it is assumed that you kept a copy of the *!RunImage* program from *OurTask* after Listing 7.1 had been added, and Listing 9.1 should be added to this.

There is one possible problem before we can run the program, however. In its earlier incarnation the three radio icons were created first and therefore were given icon handles of 0-2 by the Wimp. But if you have followed the order described in this chapter, they will probably have icon handles of 2-4. You will therefore need to make one further change to the window in FormEd, and renumber these icons as 0-2. At the same time, make sure that the three text icons which hold the temperature values have numbers of 5-7, and the coloured bar is icon number 3.

Listing 9.1

```
  160 DIM block% 500,imenu% 99,smenu% 99,limits%(2,2)
  165 DIM mainind% 150,name% 11
  200 file%=OPENIN"<Obey$Dir>.Sprites"
  205 size%=EXT#file%+4:CLOSE#file%
  210 DIM sparea% size%
  215 !sparea%=size%:sparea%!8=16
  220 SYS "OS_SpriteOp",&10A,sparea%,"<Obey$Dir>.Sprit
es"
  230 SYS "Wimp_OpenTemplate",,"<Obey$Dir>.Templates"
  235 $name%="Main"
  240 SYS "Wimp_LoadTemplate",,block%,mainind%,mainind
%+150,-1,name%,0
  245 block%!64=1:block%!208=sparea%
  250 block%!112=1:block%!144=1:block%!176=1
  255 SYS "Wimp_CreateWindow",,block% TO whandle%
  260 SYS "Wimp_CloseTemplate"
  530
 1530 WHEN whandle%:IF block%!8<>2 THEN
 1540 iconsel%=block%!16:PROCupdate
```

```
1550 ENDIF
1560 ENDCASE
2612 PROCupdate
2800 DEF PROCupdate
2810 !block%=whandle%:FOR i%=5 TO 7
2820 block%!4=i%:SYS "Wimp_GetIconState",,block%
2830 $(block%!28)=STR$limits%(iconsel%,7-i%)
2840 block%!8=0:block%!12=0
2850 SYS "Wimp_SetIconState",,block%
2860 NEXT
2870 ENDPROC
2880 :

Delete 2890-3080
```

Lines 200-220 set up a sprite area and load our *Sprites* file into it (see Appendix C for more details on sprite areas, and Appendix B for an explanation of *Obey$Dir*). Next we must load the window template and create the window (lines 230-260). Three SWI calls are required to handle templates. The first of these is **Wimp_OpenTemplate** (&400D9), which takes just one parameter: the full pathname of the template file in R1. This opens the file ready for the templates to be loaded into the program. Having done this, you must then call **Wimp_LoadTemplate** (&400DB), followed immediately by a call to **Wimp_CreateWindow** , for each window that you wish to load and create. The parameter block for **Wimp_LoadTemplate** is shown in Figure 9.4.

On entry:
R1 = pointer to user buffer for template
R2 = pointer to workspace for indirected data
R3 = pointer to end of indirected workspace
R4 = 256-byte font reference array (-1 for no fonts)
R5 = pointer to template identifier (must be 12 bytes word-aligned)
R6 = position to search from (0 for first call)

On exit:
R2 = pointer to remaining indirected workspace
R6 = position of next entry (0 if no match found)

Figure 9.4
Parameter block for SWI "Wimp_LoadTemplate" (&400DB)

Once this has all been done, the file is closed again using **Wimp_CloseTemplate** (&400DA). This latter call requires no parameters since an application can only have one template file open at any one time.

The parameter block in Figure 9.4 requires a little explanation. The buffer pointed to in R1 will hold the complete window definition as it is loaded in from the template file. This will have exactly the same format as a standard window definition block as shown in Figure 2.3 in Chapter 2. Note that it will contain all the icon definitions in the window as well (from block+88 onwards in the window definition) - when using templates we do not need to create the icons separately with **Wimp_CreateIcon**. Programs usually use the same parameter block for this buffer as for most of the other SWI calls - i.e. *block%* in *PlateTest*. It must be big enough for the largest window to be loaded, however, and we will show you how to calculate its size in a moment.

R2 holds a pointer to a block of memory which the Wimp will use to store any indirected data associated with the window, either for icons or for the title bar. Whereas the buffer in R1 is a transient store for each window definition between loading in the template and creating the window, the buffer in R2 is a *permanent* store for all the indirected data from every window thus created. The Wimp will allocate space in this buffer for each indirected icon in turn, according to the length required, and will create the icon with its indirection pointer pointing to the correct address. Because the task itself does not know the exact address of each individual icon's text (as it would if the icon were created within the program), you would normally use **Wimp_GetIconState** to find it out when necessary, as described in Chapter 5.

If you are loading more than one window template, you can either use a single block of indirected workspace for them all, in which case it must be large enough to hold *all* the indirected data from every window created from templates, or you can reserve a separate block for each window. The latter method is probably easier. In our program we are only loading one template, and we have called the pointer to the block *mainind%*, so if you wish to experiment by adding a template of your own for the program's other window (the info box), you could reserve a second block at, say, *infoind%*.

The end of the indirected workspace (i.e. the highest address available plus 1) is passed in R3. If this is not large enough to hold all the data, a "Window definition will not fit" error is generated when the program is run.

The name passed to **Wimp_LoadTemplate** in R5 is a pointer to a further buffer containing the identifier you gave the window when it was created in FormEd. Note that this buffer *must* be 12 bytes long, so it is no good just passing the identifier itself as a string at R5 as you can usually do with SWI calls, or odd things may happen when you load the template.

On exit from the call, the block whose address was supplied in R1 now holds the complete window definition for use by **Wimp_CreateWindow**, while R2 now points to the start of the remaining indirected workspace. In other words, if the first call to **Wimp_LoadTemplate** results in 20 bytes of indirected data being put into the workspace (including terminators), on exit R2 will point to an address 20 bytes higher than on entry. If you are using one block of memory for all your indirected data, this new address can then be passed in R2 when the next call to **Wimp_LoadTemplate** is made, and so on until all the templates have been loaded.

Before we can use this SWI call with confidence, we need to ensure that the block pointed to in R1 is large enough. If it is not, the data from the template file will overwrite some other part of memory and most likely cause the program to crash when it is run. No error would be generated at the time of loading the template, since the Wimp cannot know how much memory you have reserved for the block. Failing to make a block large enough for templates is a common cause of problems when developing programs, and can take a lot of time to track down since the problem may not manifest itself immediately.

The window definition block (in our case *block%*) is used for each window in turn, so it only needs to be big enough for the largest definition in the template file. This is calculated by taking the 88 bytes needed for the window definition itself and adding 32 bytes for each icon defined in the window. This is not quite the end of the story, though, since the Wimp also uses the block as a temporary store for indirected data before transferring it to the indirected workspace. So the block size must be:

88 + 32*number of icons + size of all indirected data in window

Remember to include a terminator for each string as well as the actual text itself, and also to include the window title bar if this is indirected. If you have designed your window roughly in accordance with the steps outlined in this chapter, a block of 500 bytes should be sufficient for the window definition, and one of 150 for the indirected workspace. These are the values we have used in lines 160 (*block%*) and 165 (*mainind%*) respectively. We have also dimensioned a small additional buffer, *name%*, to hold the identifier name.

USING SPRITES FROM MORE THAN ONE AREA

In our window we have used sprites both from the Wimp pool and our own sprite file. In order to do this we must follow certain rules. The window definition block contains a pointer to a global sprite area for the whole window (at block+64), and the Wimp will normally use this pointer when displaying sprites in any icons in that window. However, we have seen that indirected sprite-only icons can have a pointer of their own (see Figure 5.6) which, if present, will override the global pointer. We have made use of this facility in *PlateTest* in order to use sprites from two separate areas.

In line 245 we have set the global pointer to 1 (for the Wimp pool), and the pointer for icon number 3 (the coloured bar) to *sparea%*. The formula for setting the sprite area pointer for any given icon is as follows:

```
block%!(88+icon%*32+24)=sparea%
```

where *icon%* is the icon number and *sparea%* is the start of the sprite area. This line must of course be repeated for any other icons which are to use the same sprite area. Sharp-eyed readers may have noticed that we have addressed the word at byte 24 of the icon block, whereas Figure 5.6 shows the sprite pointer at byte 28. This is because the data in the icon block as supplied to **Wimp_CreateIcon** is displaced by 4 bytes to make space for the window handle; when we are using templates, the icons are created along with the window and each icon block is just 32 bytes long, since we no longer need to specify the window handle.

In fact, if you are using a few Wimp pool sprites together with some sprites of your own, as we have done here, you may find it preferable to put *all* the sprites into your *Sprites* file (including duplicates of any Wimp pool sprites). This file can then be loaded into the user sprite area at *sparea%*, the global pointer at block+64 can be set to this area, and you can mix text-plus-sprite and sprite-only icons, indirected and non-indirected, quite freely without any problems.

If the template file holds further window definitions, these can be loaded and created in turn by repeating lines 240-250 for each window. Once you are satisfied that the program is working correctly as listed here, you might like to try designing a template for the info box and amending the program to load it in, instead of creating it directly as we are doing at present.

As for the rest of the program, the only alteration necessary to enable it to run with templates is to include the new procedure *PROCupdate*. Originally, the display of the temperature values was handled by our redraw loop, but now we are using icons instead. This means that each time one of the radio icons is clicked, or the temperature scale is altered from the menu, we must reset the temperature values by using **Wimp_SetIconState**. *PROCupdate* (lines 2800-2870) is quite straightforward and you should have no difficulty working out exactly what it does.

As you get used to developing your own applications, you will find that FormEd becomes an indispensable tool. In order to explore its versatility, we suggest that you might like to try substituting templates for some of the window definitions we created in other listings in this book, and amending the programs to load them instead of using the original window and icon creation routines. You will probably find it helpful to have Chapters 2 & 5 of this book to hand as you experiment, in order to refresh your memory on the details of the theory as you go. With a little practice you could soon be designing windows as smart and attractive as those used by many commercial applications.

10. Printer Drivers and Outline Fonts

Printer drivers - Internal co-ordinates - The print job - Drawing the page - Colour translation - Outline fonts - Displaying outline fonts - Printing outline fonts - Epilogue

We are now approaching the end of our tour of the Wimp's complexities. In this final chapter, we will consider how to get a multi-tasking application to send its output to a printer. We will also take a brief look at the use of outline fonts for both screen and printer output, since the use of these fonts can greatly enhance the attractiveness and versatility of your textual displays.

PRINTER DRIVERS

By using a system of standardised RISC OS printer drivers, Acorn has made the provision of hardcopy a relatively painless affair for programmers. Without these drivers, each application would need to incorporate separate driver routines for each of the printer types with which the software might be used. Instead a uniform interface is provided with which to communicate - one which we might call a "virtual printer". This means that any application which uses the RISC OS drivers for printing will work with any new printer that might appear, provided that there is an appropriate printer driver available (but that is not the responsibility of the application).

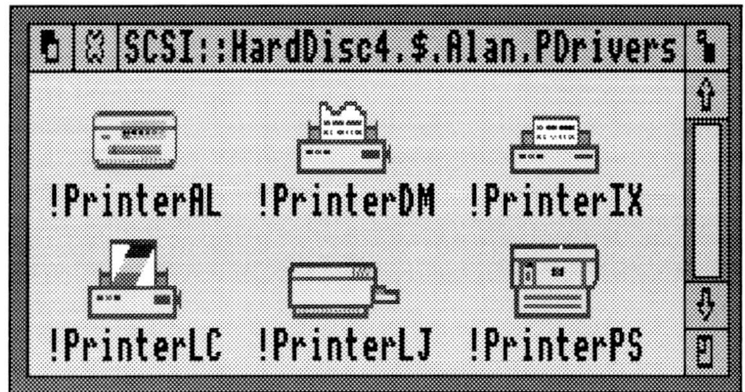

A selection of RISC OS printer drivers

In the first part of this chapter we will look at the way in which Wimp applications can access the drivers to produce hardcopy. Before we start, however, we need to differentiate between text and graphics printing, since the printer drivers have separate routines to handle each type, and each is quite different from the other.

A typical dot matrix printer (and any other printer which can simulate a dot matrix, usually by having an Epson emulation built in) operates in one of two distinct ways. For normal text printing, ASCII characters are sent to the printer, which looks up the definition of each character in its own ROM and prints the result on the page. Styles such as italics and bold, and in some cases other fonts, are built into the printer's ROM and accessed by a sequence of control codes. The important thing to realise is that the application merely sends the printer the ASCII code of the character; the exact representation of it is built into the printer itself.

With graphics printing, on the other hand, the application tells the printer to place a sequence of individual dots on the page, which may be a representation of an ASCII character or they may represent a graphic image. In this mode, it is entirely up to the application to determine what dots are to appear where. The interface to the RISC OS printer drivers which we will describe in this chapter assumes that this is the mode of operation which will be used.

In broad terms, the code to send an image to a printer driver to create a single page is similar to that used to redraw a Wimp window. This is quite logical, since the primary purpose of the driver is to reproduce on paper what you see on screen (though you can in fact send *any* image to the printer whether it appears on screen or not, provided you follow the correct procedure). A WHILE loop is normally used in which the printer driver repeatedly returns the co-ordinates of a rectangle whose contents the application must draw. This continues until the driver says that it has had enough. Preparations are then made to repeat the procedure for the next page, and so on until the end of the document.

In contrast to window redraw routines, however, the application must give the co-ordinates of one or more sections of the page to be drawn before the WHILE loop is entered, and must say whereabouts on the page they are to be reproduced. A single section could cover an entire page, or a page might be made up of a number of smaller rectangles. Since each rectangle can contain any combination of objects (text, graphics or sprites), great flexibility is possible. Figure 10.1 expands the process in pseudo code.

```
Check that a driver is installed
Call PDriver_PageSize to obtain dimensions of printable area etc.
Call PDriver_SelectJob to initiate the process

FOR page=1 TO total
  Make one or more calls to PDriver_GiveRectangle
     to nominate areas to be printed on this page
  Call PDriver_DrawPage to begin drawing process
  WHILE more
    Draw text and graphics as required
    Call PDriver_GetRectangle
  ENDWHILE
NEXT page
Call PDriver_EndJob
```

Figure 10.1
Pseudo code representation of the printer driver interface

INTERNAL CO-ORDINATES

Figure 10.1 gives the broad outline of what is going on, but the finer detail will only really emerge with reference to a real example, so in a moment we will supply a listing. Before we do so, however, it is necessary to say something about co-ordinates and units. So far in this book we have dealt with co-ordinates in terms of OS units, since these are the units used by the operating system to display objects on the screen. But printers come in all different types and in all different resolutions, and it would be a remarkable coincidence if even one printer could work in OS units. In addition to this, printing is often concerned with fonts, where it is normal to work in point sizes, one point being equal to 1/72 of an inch. So for printing and also for font handling, Acorn has devised a so-called *internal co-ordinate system*. One unit in this system is equal to a millipoint, i.e. 1/72000 of an inch. A SWI is provided to read the scaling factor between millipoints and OS units, which is normally 400 in both x and y axes (i.e. 1 OS unit = 400 millipoints).

The printer driver keeps track of paper measurements (page size, margins etc.) in millipoints, but when actually plotting an image to the driver, the task still specifies OS co-ordinates. The reason for this is to make it easier for the task to establish a relationship between the image on the screen and the image to be printed. This may seem a little confusing but it should all become clear when we study the listing below, and in fact you will not normally need to convert values between the two systems; in other words, the rectangle you print is defined in terms of OS units, but its actual position on the page is given in millipoints.

EXAMPLE PROGRAM

Listing 10.1 puts all this into practice. This should be added to *OurTask* in the usual way, and when you run the updated program you will find that when you open the window, you will see the text "Click the mouse to print" and a blue rectangle below it. Clicking on a mouse button over the window will cause something similar to be printed, provided that you have installed a printer driver first.

Although the whole process is relatively straightforward, there is quite a lot of detail to be grasped, some of which may be a little confusing initially. It will help to be thoroughly familiar with the way in which printer drivers are seen to work by the user, and of course the best way to gain this familiarity is to use them! Experimenting with hardcopy output from Draw and Paint, for example, is a good way to see the process in action. It goes without saying that if at first you find the detail in this chapter daunting, do persevere and re-read anything which is unclear.

Listing 10.1

```
 165 DIM trans% 16,rect% 16,plotat% 8
 200 whandle%=FNcreate_window(100,300,500,400,0,0,&870
00002,"Print test")
 1525 WHEN whandle%:PROCprint
 2843 SYS "Wimp_SetColour",11
 2845 MOVE ox%+16,oy%-16
 2848 PRINT "Click mouse to print"
 2850 SYS "Wimp_SetColour",8
 2855 RECTANGLE FILL ox%+40,oy%-300,400,200
 5000 DEF PROCprint
 5010 OSCLI ("RMEnsure PDriver 0 ERROR 255 No printer
driver  installed")
 5020 SYS "Hourglass_On"
 5030 pf%=OPENOUT("printer:")
 5040 SYS "PDriver_SelectJob",pf%,"Test job"
 5050 LOCAL ERROR
 5060 ON ERROR LOCAL:RESTORE ERROR:SYS "PDriver_AbortJ
ob",pf%:CLOSE#pf%:SYS "Hourglass_Off":PROCreport(REPOR
T$,1):ENDPROC
 5070 SYS "PDriver_PageSize" TO ,w%,h%,l%,b%,r%,t%
 5080 !rect%=0:rect%!4=0
 5090 rect%!8=500:rect%!12=400
```

```
5100 !trans%=1<<16:trans%!4=0
5110 trans%!8=0:trans%!12=1<<16
5120 !plotat%=l%+144000:plotat%!4=b%+144000
5130 SYS "PDriver_GiveRectangle",0,rect%,trans%,plota
t%,&DDDDDD00
5140 SYS "PDriver_DrawPage",1,block%,0,0 TO more%
5150 WHILE more%
5160 SYS "ColourTrans_SetGCOL",0
5170 MOVE 16,384
5180 PRINT "Click mouse to print"
5190 SYS "ColourTrans_SetGCOL",&33333300
5200 RECTANGLE FILL 36,100,400,200
5250 SYS "PDriver_GetRectangle",,block% TO more%
5260 ENDWHILE
5270 SYS "PDriver_EndJob",pf%
5280 SYS "Hourglass_Off"
5290 RESTORE ERROR
5300 CLOSE#pf%
5310 SOUND 1,-15,70,10
5320 ENDPROC
5330 :
```

Lines 2843-2855 replace some of the existing code in *PROCredraw* to display the required text and rectangle in the window. Line 1525 adds an instruction to *PROCclick* to ensure that a mouse click over the window activates the printing process.

THE PRINT JOB

By taking a closer look at the definition of *PROCprint* (line 5000 onwards) we can see how the print job has been implemented. To start with, we have amended the main program at line 165 to dimension three small areas of memory for use with the SWI calls. Moving to *PROCprint* itself, *RMEnsure* is used to check that a driver has been installed (line 5010). Note that driver modules still remain installed even after you select *Quit* from the driver's control application on the icon bar - only the application is removed.

If all is well, the hourglass is then turned on using SWI **Hourglass_On** (&406C0). Lines 5030 and 5040 initiate the printing job. The first opens a file to the printer, which is the preferred way of handling printer output, while the second calls SWI **PDriver_SelectJob** (&80145). This SWI requires the file handle of the printer file in R0, and a pointer to a name for the job in R1.

This suspends the current print job if there is one, and renders the nominated job current. The name supplied with the job is used in different ways by different printer drivers. Some will ignore it, while the PostScript driver, for example, includes it in the PostScript header which it generates.

Before going any further our procedure needs to set up a local error handler. This is necessary because we will have to abort the print job if any error occurs while printing is in progress. The latter is achieved with a call to SWI **PDriver_AbortJob** (&80149) with the file handle in R0. The hourglass must also be removed by a call to **Hourglass_Off**.

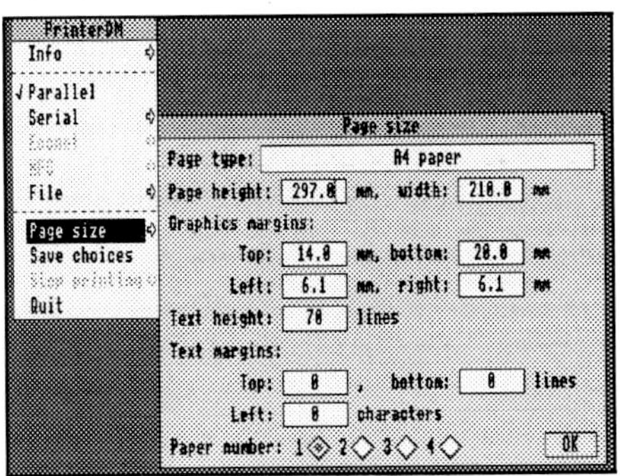

Figure 10.2
A printer driver's **Page size** *dialogue box*

The next thing we must do is to find out the current size of the page and the margin settings. If you are not familiar with using the RISC OS printer drivers we suggest that you install one and take a look at the menu options. One of these will be *Page size*, and moving the pointer across this entry will open a dialogue box (see Figure 10.2) giving details of the current page size and margin settings. These values can be read by calling SWI **PDriver_PageSize**, and the information returned by this call is shown in Figure 10.3.

R1 = x size of paper, including margins
R2 = y size of paper, including margins
R3 = left margin
R4 = bottom margin
R5 = right margin
R6 = top margin

All units are in millipoints.
R3-R6 are relative to the bottom left-hand corner of the page

Figure 10.3
Information returned by SWI "PDriver_PageSize" (&80143)

The page size data is read at line 5070. In fact, we are only using the left and bottom margins in our program at the moment, but we have included all the other returned parameters in line 5070 for the sake of completeness. Now we can start to tell the printer driver what to print. This process is done page by page. In the example given here, we are only printing one page, and the whole of the code from line 5080 to line 5260 is taken up with the process. If we wanted to print more pages, we would have to repeat this process for each one.

The first task is to specify all the sections we want to print on that page. In many cases we would treat the whole page as a single rectangle, but if the image we are printing is smaller than a page (the contents of a small window for example) we might restrict the rectangle to just one part of the page. There might also be some circumstances where we need to split the page up into more than one section - for example printing in two or more columns. We specify the rectangles by calling SWI **PDriver_GiveRectangle** (&8014B) for each one. The parameters for this call are shown in Figure 10.4.

R0 = rectangle identification word
R1 = pointer to 4-word block containing rectangle to be plotted in OS units
R2 = pointer to 4-word block containing transformation table
R3 = pointer to 2-word block containing plot position in millipoints
R4 = background colour for rectangle in the form &bbggrr00

Figure 10.4
Parameters supplied to SWI "PDriver_GiveRectangle" (&8014B)

The identification word in R0 is a value of our own choosing, and is reported back to the application when the Wimp requests that it must be plotted. This enables us to keep track of which rectangle is being requested. Since there is only one rectangle in our task we have supplied a value of zero.

The block pointed to by R1 supplies the co-ordinates in OS units of the rectangle which the task wishes to plot. It is important to realise that these co-ordinates bear no relation to any point on the printed page; they are for your own use in determining what to plot in the redraw loop. In other words, if you are drawing a specific section of a window on screen, you could give the screen co-ordinates in the call to **PDriver_GiveRectangle**, and then your redraw code would plot objects using the same co-ordinates as you would use to plot on screen. This enables you to use the same redraw loop for both screen and printer output, which makes a great deal of sense for WYSIWYG printing. If on the other hand the printed image does not necessarily relate directly to a screen image, you would normally specify the left and bottom co-ordinates as zero, and the right and top co-ordinates as the width and height of the rectangle you are plotting.

In other words, as far as the printer driver is concerned the values given in this block merely determine the size of the rectangle; the co-ordinates themselves are for your own use, not the driver's. The actual position of this rectangle on the paper is given in millipoints in the block whose address is in R3. If this is a little unclear then study what we have done in the listing. At lines 5080-5090 we have specified a rectangle 500 OS units wide by 400 OS units high, whose base point (i.e. the bottom left corner) is at co-ordinate 0,0. We could make this co-ordinate 100,100; 600,800; 345,678; or whatever we choose, provided that when we draw our image in the redraw loop, we plot it relative to the implied position of co-ordinate 0,0. You will see how this works when we look at our redraw loop. At line 5120 we have specified the actual position on paper as *l%*+144000, *b%*+144000; in other words, 2 inches in from the left margin and 2 inches up from the bottom margin.

To make this a little clearer, suppose that the rectangle we want to print is a window on the screen 400 OS units square with its bottom left-hand corner at screen co-ordinate 100,200. Within this is a line of text 50 OS units from the left and 150 OS units from the bottom of the window. We could just tell the printer driver that the rectangle starts at 0,0 and finishes at 400,400, and then during the redraw loop we would plot the text at 50,150. However, for greater efficiency we could use the same code for both screen redraw and printing. In this case we would give the co-ordinates of the rectangle to the printer driver as 100,200 and 500,600, and the text would now be plotted at 150,350, exactly as it would be on the screen. Whichever method we use, the actual position of the rectangle on the paper is still determined by the values pointed to by R3, not by the co-ordinates pointed to by R1.

To recap, the rectangle is placed on the paper at a precise position using millipoints; objects are drawn within the rectangle using OS co-ordinates relative to the real or implied position of co-ordinate 0,0. This is a very simple relationship once it is understood, and if it still seems confusing we would suggest that you re-read the above section carefully and study what we have done in the listing.

Unfortunately, to compound the complexity there appears to have been a bug in the RISC OS 2 printer drivers (except *PrinterPS*). It makes sense to plot the rectangle relative to the margins since we do not know what value these will be set to. It seems that the effect of the bug, however, is to subtract the current margin settings from the values pointed to by R3. This means that if you do what we have done here and give the value as left margin plus two inches, the rectangle will *always* be plotted two inches from the left-hand edge of the paper regardless of the current margin setting. If you want to ensure that the rectangle is relative to the margins, you would need to alter line 5120 as follows:

```
5120 !plotat%=2*l%+144000:plotat%!4=2*b%+144000
```

The printer drivers in RISC OS 3 work correctly, however, so if you are using the newer operating system you can leave line 5120 as it is in the listing in order to print relative to the margin.

The block pointed to by R2 supplies a so-called transformation table which will be applied to the rectangle. It uses the following transformation:

x'=(x * R2!0 + y * R2!8)/2^16
y'=(x * R2!4 + y * R2!12)/2^16

In our program we have used a unit transformation (lines 5100-5110) so that the rectangle appears size for size, but it is possible to shrink, expand or rotate it by altering the values supplied. Note, however, that all standard drivers except the PostScript driver reject all but the simplest transformations, and disallow any rotational element, throwing up an error box.

What this means in practice is that unless you are using a PostScript driver, you should leave the values at *trans%*+4 and *trans%*+8 as zero, since these values determine the rotational transformation. However, you can experiment with the other two values; the value at *trans%*+0 will scale in the x direction, and *trans%*+12 in the y direction. You should find that doubling the value will double the size of the image, while halving it will have the opposite effect. For example, try the following amendments and compare the results with the original program:

```
5100 trans%!0=1<<15:trans%!4=0
5110 trans%!8=0:trans%!12=1<<15
```

The final parameter supplied to **PDriver_GiveRectangle**, in R4, is the palette to be used when drawing the background of the nominated rectangle. This and all other associated palette data is supplied in the form:

&bbggrr00

The quantity of blue is given by *bb*, the quantity of green by *gg*, and so on. White - or blank paper - is made up of 100% of each of the component colours, just as it would be on screen, and is therefore &FFFFFF00. The two zeros at the end are unused, and the lower four bits of each colour should be a copy of the top four bits. Thus a mid-grey halftone might be given by:

&88888800

This might all seem very complex at first, but as always with the Wimp, it does become quite straightforward in use. Provided that you study the example program carefully, and if possible experiment with it to create your own printed output, you should find that using the printer drivers is no more difficult than drawing an image on the screen.

As we mentioned earlier, any number of rectangles may be specified for a given printed page, although we have only used one in the example. Any others should be added immediately after the first, resetting the parameter blocks as required and calling **PDriver_GiveRectangle** for each one.

Next we begin the plotting loop itself. This takes the form of a single call to SWI **PDriver_DrawPage** (&8014C) followed by a WHILE loop which makes repeated calls to SWI **PDriver_GetRectangle** (&8014D). As you can see, this is analogous to the **Wimp_RedrawWindow - Wimp_GetRectangle** loop used in redrawing a window, as described in Chapter 7. The parameters to be supplied to **PDriver_DrawPage** are shown in Figure 10.5.

On entry:
R0 = number of copies to print
R1 = pointer to 4-word block to receive rectangle to print
R2 = page sequence number within document, or zero
R3 = zero, or pointer to page number string

On exit:
R0 = non-zero if more rectangles required
R2 = rectangle identification word

Figure 10.5
Parameters used with SWI "PDriver_DrawPage" (&8014C)

If zero is returned in R0, then printing is finished and the task can proceed to the last actions required, which are to end the job and turn off the hourglass, as described below.

If R0 is non-zero, however, then the rectangle whose co-ordinates are in the block pointed to by R1 must be plotted. These co-ordinates are in OS units.

R2 and R3 are not particularly important, and are included primarily for the use of the PostScript driver. For our purposes we can leave these as zero.

DRAWING THE PAGE

The actual plotting of the image on the page is done in exactly the same way as redrawing a window, using commands such as MOVE, DRAW, PRINT, RECTANGLE and so on. The co-ordinates used with these commands are relative to the implied origin for the co-ordinates which were given in the call to **PDriver_GiveRectangle**, as we described earlier. In other words, to start drawing from a point 16 OS units in from the left and 120 OS units up from the bottom of your nominated rectangle, you should use a command such as MOVE 16,120 if you gave 0,0 as the values at line 5080, or MOVE 270,616 if you gave the values as 254,496 and so on. Any part of the image which is outside the rectangle will be clipped by the printer driver.

Just as with window redraw, you can calculate which part of the image to plot from the rectangle co-ordinates returned by **PDriver_DrawPage**, or you can take the easy way out and just draw the whole lot each time, relying on the driver to clip the unwanted parts. For a complex image, though, the latter approach would be very inefficient. In our program we have chosen the lazy way since our image is a simple one and for demonstration purposes it is better to avoid a lot of extra code.

The plotting loop is at lines 5140-5260, and is just like the contents of the equivalent window redraw loop except that colours are set using SWI **ColourTrans_SetGCOL** (&40743) rather than **Wimp_SetColour**. This ensures that accurate colour representation takes place in a manner independent of the current screen mode (see the section on colour translation below). Colours are again supplied in palette format, as described above.

If we have any more pages to print in our document (which is not the case here), we must now go through the whole process again from nominating a rectangle or rectangles to plotting the image via the plotting loop. Finally, when the whole job is finished, we call SWI **PDriver_EndJob** (&80148) with the file handle in R0, and turn off the hourglass using SWI **Hourglass_Off** (&406C1).

COLOUR TRANSLATION

We have not mentioned the ColourTrans module before now, so it is worth introducing it at this point. As you will be aware, different screen modes on the Archimedes can handle different numbers of colours; for example, mode 12 has 16 colours while mode 15 has 256. However, as we have stressed before, applications should always be mode-independent - i.e. they should not make any assumptions about the mode in use, which should be entirely at the discretion of the user. One of the problems this raises is that of colour, since the range of colours available in one mode is not necessarily going to match those in another. For this reason Acorn has provided the ColourTrans module, whose job is to translate colours from one mode to another. If a colour is defined in palette form, as described above, then ColourTrans will find the nearest match among the colours available in the current mode.

Conversely, as here, ColourTrans can be used to set a specific output colour irrespective of the current mode. This is not of much use for displaying on the screen, since the screen display is of course restricted to the current mode colours! But when using a printer driver, it allows a specific colour or shade to be set even if the current mode does not support that colour. And in any event, **Wimp_SetColour**, as we discovered when we first met the SWI in Chapter 7, can only set one of the standard 16 Wimp colours.

RISC OS 3 has ColourTrans built into the operating system ROM, but RISC OS 2 does not, so with the earlier operating system it is necessary to ensure that ColourTrans is loaded before trying to use the SWIs. You should therefore include the following lines in *OurTask*'s *!Run* file:

```
RMEnsure ColourTrans 0.51 RMLoad System:Modules.Col
ours
RMEnsure ColourTrans 0.51 Error You need ColourTran
s 0.51 or later
```

This assumes that the ColourTrans module (the file is called *Colours*) is in your *!System.Modules* directory.

OUTLINE FONTS

Up to now we have only considered the use of the system font when writing text in a task window. In this final section of the book, we will take a brief look at the use of outline fonts for both screen displays and for printed output. The support provided by RISC OS for outline fonts is considerable, and it is not possible to cover all aspects of the topic in this book. Once again, you are referred to the PRM for a full description of the use of fonts and the Outline Font Manager.

There are 34 SWIs associated with the font manager (38 in RISC OS 3), but we shall concentrate on just four of these. Here is a typical sequence of calls which could be used to display a piece of text in one of the outline fonts:

SWI Font_FindFont
SWI Font_SetFont
SWI Font_Paint
SWI Font_LoseFont

The first "opens" the font in the size required. The second establishes this as the currently selected font and size. The required text is then painted on the screen with the third SWI, and finally the font is "closed". If the program is operating in the Wimp environment then the sequence is more complex because, as always when redrawing Wimp task windows, a WHILE loop must be used to redraw the rectangles requested by the Wimp. In addition, although there is a SWI call **Font_SetPalette** to set the font colours, we cannot use this because it will corrupt the Desktop palette. Instead we must set the font palette by other means, as we shall see when we come to explain the program listing below.

EXAMPLE PROGRAM

To see how this works out in practice, we will turn to a real example. Listing 10.2 should be added to *OurTask* in the usual way, and has the effect of replacing the redraw and print procedures. When run, the updated program will display outline fonts within the task's window, and send text in outline fonts to the printer when asked to do so. As always when using outline fonts you should ensure that sufficient memory has been allocated for the font cache, either by pressing F12 to get to the command line and typing:

```
Configure FontSize <size>
```

followed by a reset, or by dragging the slider bar in the Task Manager's *Tasks* window. The example here makes use of some fairly large fonts, and you should if possible allocate around 128K to minimise file access during redraws. Note that the listing assumes that you have Trinity and Homerton in your *!Fonts* directory - if not, you should substitute the names in the listing with fonts that you do have.

Note that you must have the *Outline* Font Manager in your computer. This is supplied as standard with RISC OS 3, but the font manager and fonts provided on the Application Discs with RISC OS 2 were of the older bitmap type. Outline fonts and the Outline Font Manager have been separately available for some time, and are normally supplied when you buy a font pack or an application such as a DTP package.

Listing 10.2

```
 30 REM Updated to Chapter 10
 120 PROCclosedown
 820 PROCclosedown
 200 whandle%=FNcreate_window(100,300,800,400,0,0,&870
00002,"Font test")
 410 SYS "Font_FindFont",,"Trinity.Medium",320,320 TO
f1%
 420 SYS "Font_FindFont",,"Homerton.Medium",960,960 TO
f2%
 430 SYS "Font_FindFont",,"Trinity.Bold",1920,1920 TO
f3%
 1200 IF title$="Font test" block%?35=0 ELSE block%?35
=1
 1900 DEF PROCclosedown
 1910 SYS "Font_LoseFont",f1%
 1920 SYS "Font_LoseFont",f2%
 1930 SYS "Font_LoseFont",f3%
 1940 SYS "Wimp_CloseDown"
 1950 ENDPROC
 1960 :
 2843 SYS "Wimp_SetFontColours",,0,7
 2845 SYS "Font_SetFont",f1%
 2848 SYS "Font_Paint",,"Click mouse to print",16,ox%,
oy%-100
 2850 SYS "Font_SetFont",f2%
 2855 SYS "Font_Paint",,"60 pt Swiss",16,ox%,oy%-280
 5090 rect%!8=960:rect%!12=800
 5120 !plotat%=l%+72000:plotat%!4=b%+288000
 5130 SYS "PDriver_GiveRectangle",0,rect%,trans%,plota
t%,&FFFFFF00
 5170 RECTANGLE 4,4,952,792
 5180 SYS "ColourTrans_SetFontColours",,&FFFFFF00,0,6
 5190 SYS "Font_SetFont",f1%
 5200 SYS "Font_Paint",,"Trinity 20 point",16,12,700
 5210 SYS "Font_SetFont",f2%
 5220 SYS "Font_Paint",,"SWISS 60 pt",16,12,400
 5230 SYS "Font_SetFont",f3%
 5240 SYS "Font_Paint",,"Trinity",16,12,100
```

The first thing to be done is to open the fonts by using **Font_FindFont** in lines 410-430 (and to close them again when the task terminates by placing the calls to **Font_LoseFont** in a new procedure *PROCclosedown* at lines 1900-1950). The parameters for **Font_FindFont** are shown in Figure 10.6, while for **Font_LoseFont** (&40082) you simply put the font handle in R0. You will notice from Figure 10.6 that the size values are specified in 16ths of a point; looking at lines 410-430 you will see that we have therefore specified point sizes and font widths of 20, 60 and 120 for our three fonts respectively.

On entry:
R1 = pointer to font name
R2 = x point size * 16 (i.e. 16ths of a point)
R3 = y point size * 16 (i.e. 16ths of a point)

On exit:
R0 = font handle

Figure 10.6
Details of SWI "Font_FindFont" (&40081)

DISPLAYING OUTLINE FONTS

The rest of the listing consists of the amendments to the redraw and print procedures. Once the three fonts have been opened at the start of the program we can ignore them completely until we receive a redraw request. The response to this is handled by the amendments to *PROCredraw* in lines 2843-2855. Again, for the sake of simplicity we have opted to redraw the whole window whenever we are asked to redraw any part of it. As you will see, the redraw loop consists of five separate SWI calls. The first establishes the anti-alias palette. This is then followed by two pairs of calls. The first of each of these selects a particular font, while the second paints the text at the location supplied.

To set up the palette, we have used SWI **Wimp_SetFontColours** (&400F3). The second and third parameters (R0 is not used) are the font background and foreground colours respectively. With this call, logical colour numbers are used, and it is assumed that colours 0-7 form a grey-scale sequence. This may not be the case if the Wimp palette has been altered.

We have used colours 0 and 7 - white background and black foreground, rather than the grey background used for our main window previously. The reason for this is to make the screen palette mirror the palette which will be used for hardcopy. By amending line 1200 in the listing we have ensured that the colours for the info box and save box are unchanged.

To select the font to be used with SWI **Font_Paint**, we use SWI **Font_SetFont** which takes a single parameter, the handle of the required font in R0 (as supplied by **Font_FindFont** above). The parameters for **Font_Paint** are shown in Figure 10.7.

R1 = pointer to string
R2 = plot type
R3 = x co-ordinate
R4 = y co-ordinate

The plot type in R2 is determined as follows:

Bit	**Action**
0	1 = justify text, 0 = left justify
1	1 = rub-out box required, 0 = no box
2	must be zero
3	must be zero
4	1 = OS units in R3/R4, 0 = millipoints
5-7	must be zero

Figure 10.7
Parameters for SWI "Font_Paint" (&40086)

We have used a plot type of 16, which means that the text will be left justified, with no rub-out box, and that x and y co-ordinates marking the start of text will be supplied in OS units. For details of text justification and rub-out boxes, you are referred to the PRM. A final point to note in connection with this call is that, as usual, the origin is at the top left-hand corner of the work area, so that y co-ordinates range from zero (at the top of the window) to negative values.

PRINTING OUTLINE FONTS

Depending on the quality of your printer, some quite spectacular results can be obtained by sending graphics and outline fonts to the printer drivers. Listing 10.1 earlier in this chapter did not really show what can be done, but Listing 10.2 will give you a better idea of what you can achieve. The result of clicking the mouse over the window (assuming you have a printer driver installed and a printer connected) should look something like the illustration in Figure 10.8.

Looking at the listing, you will see that the new version of *PROCprint* is very much like the old one in Listing 10.1, except that the lines falling within the redraw loop follow the style of those used in the new window redraw loop. There is one vital difference between the two, however: the anti-aliasing palette is set by using **ColourTrans_SetFontColours** rather than **Wimp_SetFontColours**. It is essential to use the former here to achieve the best conversion of the colour palette into printed output. The parameters for this call are shown in Figure 10.9.

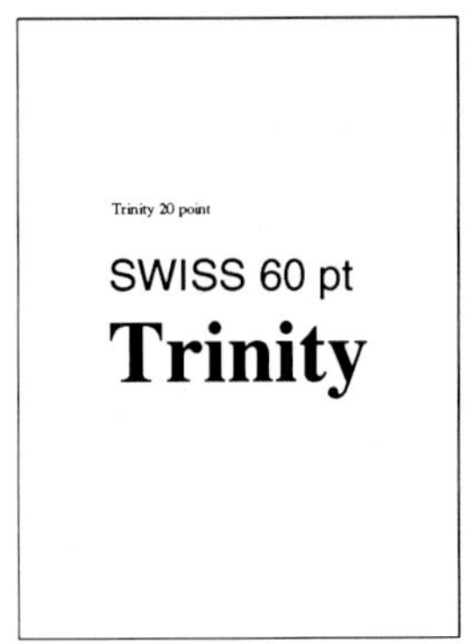

Figure 10.8
Printed output from Listing 10.2

The palette is supplied in the usual &bbggrr00 format described above, and here we have used white as the background colour and black as the foreground. The final parameter (R3) gives the number of colours to be used for the anti-alias palette (i.e. how many in-between colours are to be used), and may take values from 0-14. Now, if we are addressing the printer drivers this parameter will be ignored - you cannot perform anti-aliasing on a mono printer, because paper pixels can only be black or white (white = no dot). We have nevertheless used a value of 6 (the Wimp grey palette runs from colour 0 to colour 7, and thus has 6 in-between colours) for compatibility with screen use.

R0 = font handle (0 for current font)
R1 = background palette
R2 = foreground palette
R3 = maximum colour offset

Figure 10.9
Parameters for SWI
"ColourTrans_SetFontColours" (&4074F)

If you look at the printout produced, you will see that it is different from the screen display. It contains an additional rectangular border, and the text is different. This is easy to achieve, because we have used different code for redrawing the task's window from that which addresses the printer drivers. In many applications, however, it is vital to achieve a WYSIWYG effect. In a word processor or DTP package, for example, it would make a great deal of sense to use a single piece of code which could be called by the equivalents of *PROCredraw* and *PROCprint*. If this is the case you would normally use **ColourTrans_SetFontColours** for both screen and printer colours. In this case, the final parameter supplied with this call becomes important, since it is necessary for on-screen anti-aliasing.

There is a lot of experimentation which you could carry out using this listing as a basis, and the program could easily be extended to generate almost any kind of hardcopy. For example, it could read in a file of names and addresses and print out smart looking address labels; or you could generate graphs, bar charts, posters, or whatever - all with the same pixel perfect crispness, given of course a good quality printer.

EPILOGUE

We have now sadly reached the end of our journey through the Wimp. If you have enjoyed the trip, you will probably by now be writing your own Wimp programs and no doubt will have made many amendments to our listings in the course of your experiments. We hope you have found the book both instructive and enjoyable. There is of course much more to learn if you want to delve further into the subject - the RISC OS 2 PRM runs to over 1800 pages and the RISC OS 3 version is even larger. Nevertheless, the information we have presented here is enough to enable you to construct many quite powerful applications of your own. We hope that we have not left you floundering too often in the course of the book, but we can assure you that the Archimedes is so powerful and versatile that the satisfaction you will gain from mastering the Wimp will repay all the effort involved. Happy programming!

Appendix A. Indirection Operators

There are a number of reasons why you may need to access memory directly on an Archimedes. You might, for example, need to work with text strings longer than the 255 character limit imposed by Basic, or you may need to set up parameter blocks for use with SWI calls, as we have described in numerous places in this book. Here is how it is done.

RESERVING MEMORY

First of all you must reserve an area of memory. This is done by using the DIM statement, and you will see throughout the listings in this book that we have used this statement to reserve the memory required for our parameter blocks. As an example:

```
DIM block% 255
```

will reserve 256 bytes of RAM (i.e. one byte more than specified) for use by your program, and the variable *block%* will be assigned (by Basic) to hold the start address of this block. It is worth noting that the block is always word-aligned (i.e. the start address is always divisible by 4).

READING AND WRITING TO MEMORY

BBC Basic V (as provided on the Archimedes) has four so-called *indirection operators* for reading and writing directly to memory. The details of these are shown in Figure A.1.

Symbol	Purpose	Number of bytes
?	read/write a byte	1
!	read/write a 32-bit word	4
|	read/write a floating point value	5
$	read/write a string	0-255

Figure A.1
Basic's four indirection operators

To store a byte of value 123 at the location *block%*, use the query operator:

```
?block%=123
```

Only integers in the range 0 to 255 may be stored in this way. To display the value at *block%*, use:

```
PRINT ?block%
```

This will only work of course if you have already reserved an area of memory at *block%*.

The pling operator (!) works in a similar way:

```
!block%=100000
```

will store the value 100000 at *block%*. But now it is stored in four consecutive bytes (low byte first), thus providing a much greater range of values, namely -2147483648 to 2147483647. To display the four-byte (32 bit) value at *block%*, use:

```
PRINT !block%
```

The two operators ! and ? (but not | or $) can make use of a special so-called *dyadic* form of notation, where:

block%?4 is equivalent to **?(block%+4)**

and

block%!100 equates to **!(block%+100)**

In other words, the address is formed by adding the two values together. The value before the operator must be a variable, while the second value may be a variable, a number or a bracketed expression.

The | operator (the | key is just above the Return key) functions in a similar way to query and pling, except that it uses five consecutive bytes, and is used for treating floating point numbers. The range of these is:

-1.7×10^{38} to 1.7×10^{38}

with an accuracy of 9 significant figures.

The $ operator will store and retrieve strings. To store the string "bananas" at *block%*, use:

```
$block%="bananas"
```

The effect of this is to store ASCII "b" at *block%*, ASCII "a" at *block%+1*, and so on. A carriage return character (ASCII 13) is automatically added at the end of the string in memory (in this case at *block%+7*), but this is not echoed when the string is retrieved. Thus if you use:

```
text$=$block%
```

to read the string into *text$*, the latter will not contain a carriage return.

Finally, you might like to try the short accompanying program to demonstrate the use of each operator.

```
 10 REM >MemAccess
 20 REM Demo of indirection operators
 30 :
 40 DIM block% &100
 50 :
 60 ?block%=255
 70 block%!4=100000
 80 |(block%+8)=1.23456789876E9
 90 $(block%+13)="String storage"
100 :
110 PRINT ?block%
120 PRINT block%!4
130 PRINT |(block%+8)
140 PRINT $(block%+13)
```

Appendix B. Application Resources

The concept of application directories was devised by Acorn as a way of ensuring that all applications running under RISC OS follow a standardised pattern. This approach is beneficial for a number of reasons. Firstly, it is easier to maintain uniformity of appearance, and therefore new applications will seem more familiar to the user when they are encountered. Secondly, it provides a framework for the programmer to follow, rather than leaving each individual to go his own way in the dark. Thirdly, it allows applications to be filing-system-independent; in other words they will always work irrespective of where they are located. Fourthly, RISC OS itself can recognise an application as such, and also recognise the purpose of certain files within the application directory provided that they have been given the standard names. And finally, the resources for an individual application are collected in one place, instead of being spread around.

If you have already read Chapter 1 and followed the advice we gave you then, you should by now have an application directory called *!OurTask*, into which you have placed a *!Run* file together with the *!RunImage* program made up of the listings given in each chapter. This skeleton framework has enabled you to run the program from the Desktop, but there is much more to be said about application directories and the resources contained within them. If you open up a typical application directory belonging to a commercial application, you are likely to see quite a number of different files inside it (see Figure B.1). As well as the two we have already met, there could be files called *!Boot, !Sprites, !Help, Templates,* and *Sprites,* as well as data files called *Choices, Defaults* or whatever. Files whose names begin with "!"

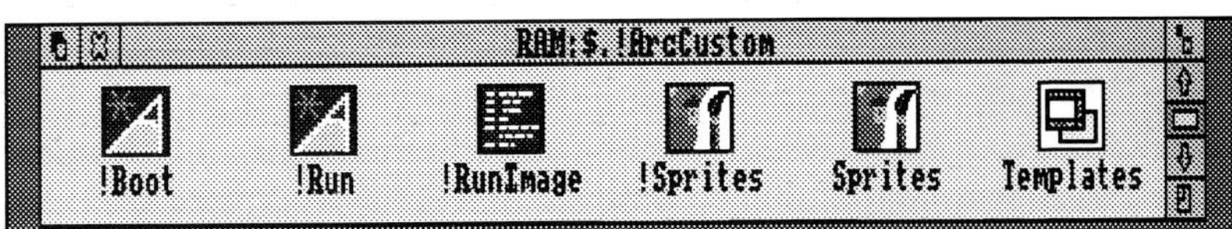

Figure B.1
A typical application directory

have a special meaning to RISC OS, while other files can have any name the application chooses but usually conform to commonly-used conventions.

THE !Run FILE

As we said in Chapter 1, when a user double-clicks on an application directory, RISC OS looks for a file called *!Run* within that directory. If this cannot be found, an error is generated, so it follows that you must provide such a file if you wish your application to be started up from the Desktop in the normal way.

!Run must always be an Obey file, which means that the list of commands it contains are commands which can be executed by the operating system. In other words, any commands which can be typed at the command line, or executed from Basic as star commands, can be included (though you do not need to include the star character itself).

You will find it useful to look through some of the *!Run* files in your collection (those belonging to Edit, Draw and Paint, for example) to see how such a file is compiled, and what kind of commands are included. Just drag the file into Edit to view it. A typical *!Run* file for a small application might look like this:

```
Set AppName$Dir <Obey$Dir>
WimpSlot -min 64K -max 64K
IconSprites <Obey$Dir>.!Sprites
Run <Obey$Dir>.!RunImage
```

We will describe what these lines do one by one, but first it is necessary to explain the meaning of that curious phrase *<Obey$Dir>*. Whenever an Obey file is executed, the full pathname of the directory which contains the file is placed by the operating system into a system variable called *Obey$Dir*. This is a very powerful feature of RISC OS which allows applications to be completely media-independent - in other words, it doesn't matter which disc or filing system they are run from because the path which points to the application is not determined until it is actually run (i.e. *Obey$Dir* is set by running *!Run*). Compare this with programs on the old BBC micro, for instance, which expect the disc to be in drive 0 and complain if it is not. It also means that all the commands in the *!Run* file can make use of *Obey$Dir* if they need to; for example, the line:

```
Run <Obey$Dir>.!RunImage
```

which we already have in our own file makes use of *Obey$Dir* to tell the operating system exactly which *!RunImage* to run (the angle brackets around the variable merely tell the operating system to substitute the current value of the variable, i.e. at this point in time the application's pathname, when it is encountered).

Now we will look at the commands themselves.

```
Set AppName$Dir <Obey$Dir>
```

sets a new system variable to the current value of *Obey$Dir*. This new variable can have any name you choose, but it is usual to use the name of the application followed by *$Dir* as we have done here. This immediately ties in the variable to your application and ensures that under most circumstances it will be unique. The reason why we might need this variable is so that we can find the path back to the application directory later on, while our task is running. If you think about it, *Obey$Dir* will change next time an Obey file is executed (for example when another application is run), and so if our task needs to look for resources within its directory (a default choices file perhaps), it cannot rely on *Obey$Dir* still pointing to the same place. For this reason, if you need to access any files at all within the application directory once your task has been installed, you must set a system variable as here, and then use this to access the file. For example:

```
file%=OPENUP("<AppName$Dir>.Choices")
```

would open up a file called *Choices* within the application directory.

```
WimpSlot -min 64K -max 64K
```

sets the size of the memory slot which will be allocated by the Wimp to the application when it is run. This should be large enough for the program itself, its variable storage area and stack, any blocks of memory reserved from within the program, and Basic's own workspace (currently from &8000-&8F00). There is no hard and fast rule on how to calculate the slot required, other than to err on the large side (if in doubt, add 16K to the size of the program plus the total of all your reserved memory blocks). If the WimpSlot is not large enough to run the program, you are likely to get an error of the form "No writable memory at this address", since the program will overrun the highest address allocated by the Wimp for its use. If the program installs, but there is not enough room for variable storage or reserved memory blocks, the error will depend on the action the program is trying to perform at the moment the memory runs out. This could be "No room for this DIM" or "Too many nested structures", for example.

```
IconSprites <Obey$Dir>.!Sprites
```

tells the Wimp to put all the sprites in the application's *!Sprites* file into the Wimp sprite pool. We will be looking at the purpose of this file in a moment. Normally this action is performed automatically whenever an application is seen for the first time in a directory display (usually by the *!Boot* file - see below), but it is wise to include the line in the *!Run* file for the simple reason that if a user runs the application from a boot sequence when the computer is started up, the directory display will not have been opened. In these circumstances, if this line is omitted from the *!Run* file, the application will be installed but the icon on the icon bar will be invisible.

```
Run <Obey$Dir>.!RunImage
```

should be the last line in the *!Run* file, and causes the *!RunImage* program to be run.

There are many other commands that may be, and often are, included in a *!Run* file. For example, modules may be loaded, filetypes may be set and so on. For most simple applications, however, the lines described here are usually adequate.

THE !Boot FILE

Most applications, though not all, have a *!Boot* file. This is executed automatically whenever an application is seen for the first time in a directory display. For this reason, it normally contains the line we saw earlier:

```
IconSprites <Obey$Dir>.!Sprites
```

If there is no boot file, then this action is performed automatically by the Wimp in any case, but if there *is* a boot file, it should always contain this line.

There are other reasons for having a boot file. If an application has been designed to recognise certain filetypes which "belong" to that application (as Draw does, for example, with Draw files), then it is useful for the sprites for these files, and the actions to be performed when the files are double-clicked, to be notified to the Wimp at the earliest possible stage. So a boot file can make sure that the Wimp has a copy of the sprites by putting them in the sprite pool as we saw above, and can also set the system variable which tells the Wimp how to proceed if a file of that type is run. This would be done with a line such as:

```
Set Alias$@RunType_nnn Run <Obey$Dir>.!RunImage %%*0
```

which ensures that when a file of type *nnn* is double-clicked, the *!RunImage* program belonging to the application which owns the boot file is run.

THE !Sprites FILE

All applications will normally have a file called *!Sprites*. It is not obligatory to have one, but since the main purpose of this file is to provide the sprite which is is used to illustrate the application both in the directory display and on the icon bar, it is advisable to include one. The file will normally contain at least one sprite called *!appname*; in other words, the same name as the application directory itself. The Wimp will then recognise this as the sprite to use in the directory display. Following Acorn's guidelines, this sprite should be created in mode 12 and should be 34x17 pixels in size. Strictly speaking, you should also provide a second, smaller sprite (17x9 pixels) called *sm!appname*, which is used when the *Small icons* option is chosen for directory displays. If the application "owns" any filetypes, the sprites for these will also be in the *!Sprites* file. For an example of this, look at Maestro; you will see that its *!Sprites* file has a sprite called *file_af1* for its file icons.

Other files which may be found inside an application directory are:

Templates this will contain window template definitions as described in Chapter 9.

Sprites this will normally contain a set of sprites which are used within the program and will be loaded into a user sprite area - see Appendix C. There may also be files called *Sprites22* and *Sprites23*, which contain sprites for use in different modes.

!Help if the Filer finds a *!Help* file within an application, it will add a *Help* option to its *Application* submenu. Choosing this option will run the file, which will normally contain descriptive text about the application.

In addition to these commonly-used resources, an application may have any other files it may need inside its directory, such as defaults to be loaded in at start-up and so on.

This appendix is only intended to give you a brief introduction to application resources. The subject is often covered in magazine articles and other publications relating to the Archimedes, as well as the PRM and Acorn's *RISC OS Style Guide*, and a greater understanding of the use of application resources can often be gained by studying the structure of various applications themselves.

Appendix C. Setting up a Sprite Area

Many programs use sprites in their window displays. These may be sprites which the programmer has designed himself, or they may be sprites which already exist, either as part of the pool of sprites built into the RISC OS ROM, or defined by some other application. In addition to the ROM pool, the Wimp maintains a second sprite pool in RAM, and this is where all sprites whose files are subject to a **IconSprites* command are put. This enables applications to place their own sprites (e.g. for directory displays, filetypes, icon bar icons etc.) into the pool so that they are always available when they need to be displayed. You can see all the sprites that are currently in both the ROM and RAM pools with the following simple program:

```
10 SYS "Wimp_BaseOfSprites" TO rom%,ram%
20 SYS "OS_SpriteOp",268,rom%,"ROMSprites"
30 SYS "OS_SpriteOp",268,ram%,"RAMSprites"
```

This program will save two sprite files in the current directory, called *ROMsprites* and *RAMsprites*. These files can then be loaded into Paint to view the sprites.

As explained in Chapter 5, it is possible to display these sprites in icons by setting the appropriate sprite area pointer to point to the Wimp pool. However, it is normally only necessary to load into the Wimp pool those sprites which are actually needed for other purposes, such as directory displays and filetypes. Every sprite loaded into the Wimp pool takes up memory, and it is not a good idea to fill the pool with sprites that are only used within your program, since they will then remain in the pool after the task is terminated, taking up valuable memory.

The recommended method of using your own sprites is to create a sprite area within the program, by reserving a block of memory and loading the sprites into it. You would then have two sprite files in your application directory: the normal *!Sprites* file would contain only those sprites which are required by the Wimp (see Appendix B for further details), while a second file would hold all those sprites which you wish to load into your own area. This can have any name you like, but is usually called *Sprites*.

The sprite area would be set up as follows:

```
file%=OPENIN"<AppName$Dir>.Sprites"
size%=EXT#file%+4:CLOSE#file%
DIM sparea% size%
!sparea%=size%:sparea%!8=16
SYS"OS_SpriteOp",&10A,sparea%,"<AppName$Dir>.Sprites"
```

The first two lines find the size of the sprite file, then the third reserves a block of memory starting at *sparea%* equal to this size plus 4 bytes for the initial word of the sprite area header, which is not saved as part of the sprite file. The sprite area is set up in the fourth line by placing the size of the area at *sparea%*, and a value of 16 at *sparea%*+8 (this value will normally always be 16 - don't worry about why for the moment). The final line then loads a file called *Sprites* from a directory pointed to by *AppName$Dir* (see Appendix B) into memory at *sparea%*. Provided that the sprite area pointers in your window and/or icon definition blocks point to *sparea%*, as described in Chapters 5 and 9, then any sprites from the file which are used in sprite icons will be displayed correctly.

A full description of **OS_SpriteOp** is outside the scope of this book, but the PRM gives all the details of its use. For all practical purposes, the lines shown above can always be added to a program in order to create a sprite area and load in a sprite file. *AppName$Dir* must of course be replaced by your own system variable (see Appendix B).

Appendix D. SWI calls described in this book

SWI call	SWI number	Introduced in Chapter
ColourTrans_SetFontColours	&4074F	10
ColourTrans_SetGCOL	&40743	10
Font_FindFont	&40081	10
Font_LoseFont	&40082	10
Font_Paint	&40086	10
Font_SetFont	&4008A	10
Hourglass_Off	&40C61	10
Hourglass_On	&40C62	10
OS_ReadModeVariable	&35	7
OS_ReadVarVal	&23	8
OS_SpriteOp	&2E	7
PDriver_AbortJob	&80149	10
PDriver_DrawPage	&8014C	10
PDriver_EndJob	&80148	10
PDriver_GetRectangle	&8014D	10
PDriver_GiveRectangle	&8014B	10
PDriver_PageSize	&80143	10
PDriver_SelectJob	&80145	10
Wimp_CloseDown	&400DD	1
Wimp_CloseTemplate	&400DA	9
Wimp_CloseWindow	&400C6	2
Wimp_CreateIcon	&400C2	5
Wimp_CreateMenu	&400D4	6
Wimp_CreateSubMenu	&400E8	6
Wimp_CreateWindow	&400C1	2
Wimp_DragBox	&400D0	8
Wimp_ForceRedraw	&400D1	7
Wimp_GetIconState	&400CE	5
Wimp_GetPointerInfo	&400CF	6
Wimp_GetRectangle	&400CA	7
Wimp_GetWindowState	&400CB	2
Wimp_Initialise	&400C0	1
Wimp_LoadTemplate	&400DB	9

Wimp_OpenTemplate	&400D9	9
Wimp_OpenWindow	&400C5	2
Wimp_Poll	&400C7	1
Wimp_ProcessKey	&400DC	3
Wimp_RedrawWindow	&400C8	7
Wimp_ReportError	&400DF	1
Wimp_SendMessage	&400E7	8
Wimp_SetColour	&400E6	7
Wimp_SetFontColours	&400F3	10
Wimp_SetIconState	&400CD	5
Wimp_UpdateWindow	&400C9	7

Appendix E. The Associated Disc

A disc to accompany this book is available from the publishers. The disc contains the application *OurTask* at each stage of its development, so that (for example) *OurTask5c* is the application as it should be if Listing 5.3 has just been added to the *!RunImage* program.

In addition to the listings from the book, the disc contains the *Wimp Function/Procedure Library*, as published in RISC User magazine from May 1992 to August/September 1992. This is a library of useful functions to enable applications to be created easily without having to write specific code to create windows, icons or menus. For example, there is a more generalised version of *FNcreate_window* which allows more parameters to be specified, which would be too complex to introduce in a tutorial book such as this. There are routines to create the most common types of icons (such as icons on the icon bar,) and a set of menu procedures which make menu creation very easy indeed. Full documentation is included on the disc.

OBTAINING THE ASSOCIATED DISC

The disc of programs described above may be obtained direct from the publisher for £4.95 inc. VAT plus £1 p&p. The disc is a 3.5" E-format disc for use on the Archimedes.

Appendix F. The Wimp Programmer's Toolkit

The Wimp Programmer's Toolkit is a collection of twelve multi-tasking utilities for use when creating Wimp applications. The applications included are as follows:

- ❑ **SpyGlass** - allows you to select any running application and display dynamically the contents of the memory allocated to it
- ❑ **Wimp Debugger** - provides a set of routines to incorporate into your application code so that debugging information can be displayed in a Wimp window while the application is running
- ❑ **Template Editor** - Acorn's FormEd for designing windows, as described in Chapter 9
- ❑ **Template File Browser** - gives detailed information on the contents of template files
- ❑ **Application Shell Generator** - creates application directories automatically
- ❑ **Menu Editor** - enables menu structures to be defined and saved as special files which can be loaded by your application
- ❑ **WimpAid** - displays information about objects under the mouse pointer, such as window handles, icon handles, co-ordinates etc.
- ❑ **Icon Bar Shell** - a program shell which allows icon bar applications to be created easily simply by appending code to one procedure
- ❑ **Desktop File Loader** - allows files to be loaded quickly to speed up editing
- ❑ **Icon Flag Generator** - calculates the value of icon flags easily
- ❑ **EasyWimp** - ready-made Wimp application shell for window-based applications
- ❑ **Wimp Message Monitor** - monitors Wimp message passing as it happens

OBTAINING THE WIMP PROGRAMMER'S TOOLKIT

The Wimp Programmer's Toolkit may be obtained direct from the publisher for £19.95 inc. VAT plus £1 p&p. There is a special price of £14.95 plus £1 p&p for subscribers to RISC User magazine.

Index